Major Muslim Nations

# JORDAN

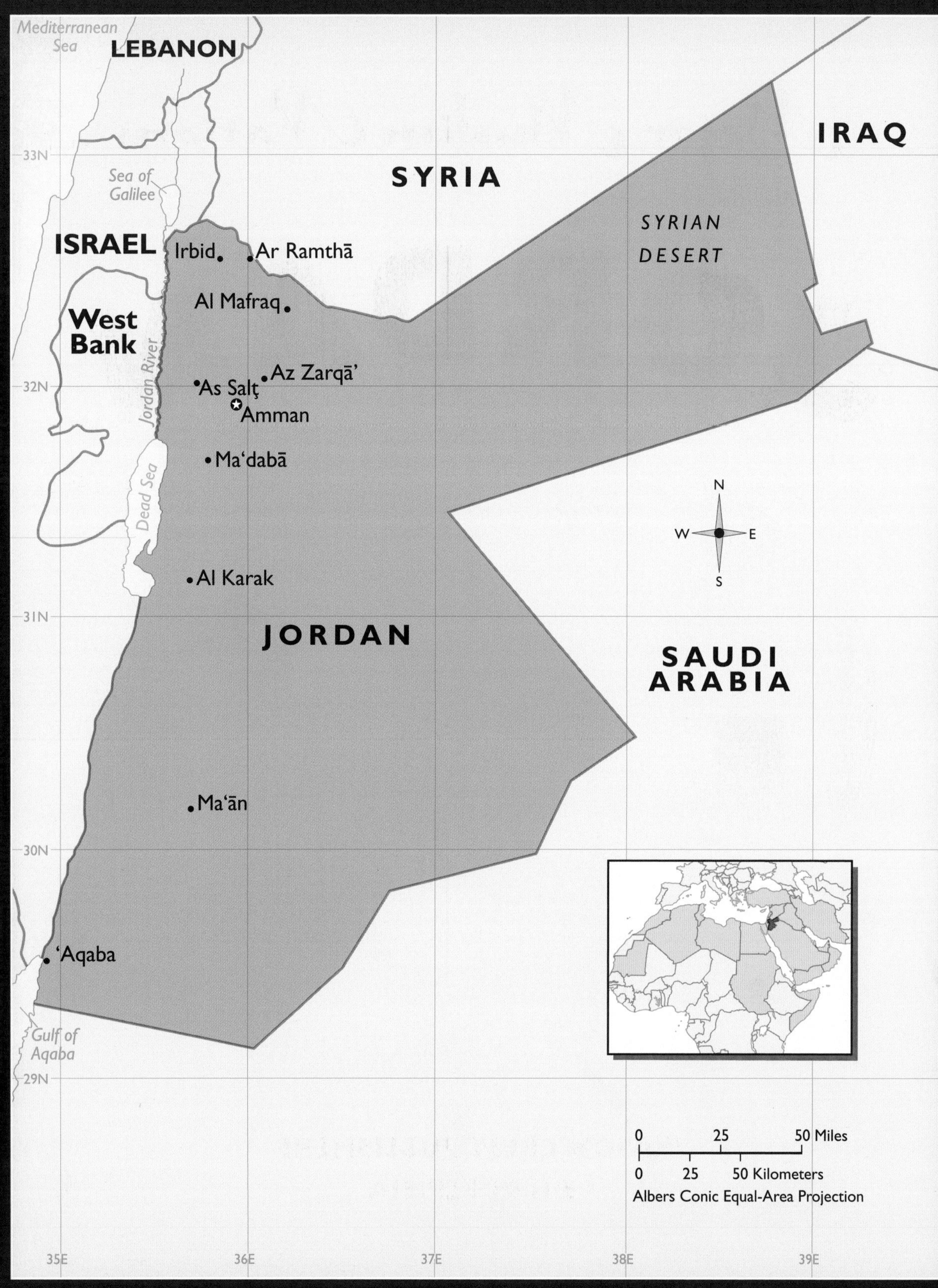

Mediterranean Sea
LEBANON
SYRIA
IRAQ
Sea of Galilee
ISRAEL
Irbid
Ar Ramthā
SYRIAN DESERT
Al Mafraq
West Bank
Jordan River
Az Zarqā'
As Salţ
Amman
Ma'dabā
Dead Sea
N
W
E
S
Al Karak
JORDAN
SAUDI ARABIA
Ma'ān
'Aqaba
Gulf of Aqaba
33N
32N
31N
30N
29N
35E
36E
37E
38E
39E
0
25
50 Miles
0
25
50 Kilometers
Albers Conic Equal-Area Projection

Major Muslim Nations

# JORDAN

ANNA CAREW-MILLER

MASON CREST PUBLISHERS
PHILADELPHIA

**Mason Crest Publishers**
370 Reed Road
Broomall, PA 19008
www.masoncrest.com


Printed and bound in the Hashemite Kingdom of Jordan.

First printing

1 3 5 7 9 8 6 4 2

Library of Congress Cataloging-in-Publication Data

Carew-Miller, Anna.
Jordan / Anna Carew-Miller.
p. cm. — (Major Muslim Nations)
Includes index.
ISBN 978-1-4222-1383-4 (hardcover) — ISBN 978-1-4222-1413-8 (pbk.)
1. Jordan—Juvenile literature. I. Title.
DS153.C37 2004
956.95—dc22
2008042169

Original ISBN: 1-59084-507-2 (hc)

# TABLE OF CONTENTS

# Major Muslim Nations

AFGHANISTAN
ALGERIA
BAHRAIN
EGYPT
INDONESIA
IRAN
IRAQ
ISLAM IN ASIA: FACTS AND FIGURES
ISLAMISM AND TERRORIST GROUPS IN ASIA
ISRAEL
JORDAN
THE KURDS
KUWAIT
LEBANON
LIBYA
MALAYSIA
MIDDLE EAST: FACTS AND FIGURES
MOROCCO
PAKISTAN
PALESTINIANS
QATAR
SAUDI ARABIA
SOMALIA
SUDAN
SYRIA
TUNISIA
TURKEY
UAE
YEMEN

Dr. Harvey Sicherman, president and director of the Foreign Policy Research Institute, is the author of such books as *America the Vulnerable: Our Military Problems and How to Fix Them* (2002) and *Palestinian Autonomy, Self-Government and Peace* (1993).

# Introduction

## by Dr. Harvey Sicherman

America's triumph in the Cold War promised a new burst of peace and prosperity. Indeed, the decade between the demise of the Soviet Union and the destruction of September 11, 2001, seems in retrospect deceptively attractive. Today, of course, we are more fully aware—to our sorrow—of the dangers and troubles no longer just below the surface.

The Muslim identities of most of the terrorists at war with the United States have also provoked great interest in Islam and the role of religion in politics. A truly global religion, Islam's tenets are held by hundreds of millions of people from every ethnic group, scattered across the globe. It is crucial for Americans not to assume that Osama bin Laden's ideas are identical to those of most Muslims, or, for that matter, that most Muslims are Arabs. Also, it is important for Americans to understand the "hot spots" in the Muslim world because many will make an impact on the United States.

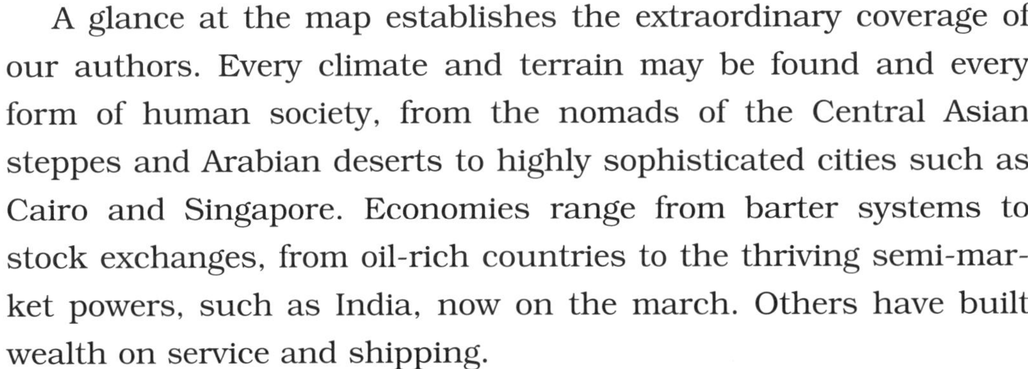

A glance at the map establishes the extraordinary coverage of our authors. Every climate and terrain may be found and every form of human society, from the nomads of the Central Asian steppes and Arabian deserts to highly sophisticated cities such as Cairo and Singapore. Economies range from barter systems to stock exchanges, from oil-rich countries to the thriving semi-market powers, such as India, now on the march. Others have built wealth on service and shipping.

The Middle East and Central Asia are heavily armed and turbulent. Pakistan is a nuclear power, Iran threatens to become one, and Israel is assumed to possess a small arsenal. But in other places, such as Afghanistan and the Sudan, the horse and mule remain potent instruments of war. All have a rich history of conflict, domestic and international, old and new.

Governments include dictatorships, democracies, and hybrids without a name; centralized and decentralized administrations; and older patterns of tribal and clan associations. The region is a veritable encyclopedia of political expression.

Although such variety defies easy generalities, it is still possible to make several observations.

First, the regional geopolitics reflect the impact of empires and the struggles of post-imperial independence. While centuries-old history is often invoked, the truth is that the modern Middle East political system dates only from the 1920s, when the Ottoman Empire dissolved in the wake of its defeat by Britain and France in World War I. States such as Algeria, Iraq, Israel, Jordan, Kuwait, Saudi Arabia, Syria, Turkey, and the United Arab Emirates did not exist before 1914—they became independent between 1920 and 1971. Others, such as Egypt and Iran, were dominated by foreign powers until well after World War II. Few of the leaders of these states were happy with the territories they were assigned or the borders, which were often drawn by Europeans. Yet the system has endured despite many efforts to change it.

A similar story may be told in South Asia. The British Raj dissolved into India and Pakistan in 1947. Still further east, Malaysia shares a British experience but Indonesia, a Dutch invention, has its own European heritage. These imperial histories weigh heavily upon the politics of the region.

The second observation concerns economics, demography, and natural resources. These countries offer dramatic geographical contrasts: vast parched deserts and high mountains, some with year-round snow; stone-hard volcanic rifts and lush semi-tropical valleys; extremely dry and extremely wet conditions, sometimes separated by only a few miles; large permanent rivers and wadis, riverbeds dry as a bone until winter rains send torrents of flood from the mountains to the sea.

Although famous historically for its exports of grains, fabrics, and spices, most recently the Muslim regions are known more for a single commodity: oil. Petroleum is unevenly distributed; while it is largely concentrated in the Persian Gulf and Arabian Peninsula, large oil fields can be found in Algeria, Libya, and further east in Indonesia. Natural gas is also abundant in the Gulf, and there are new, potentially lucrative offshore gas fields in the Eastern Mediterranean.

This uneven distribution of wealth has been compounded by demographics. Birth rates are very high, but the countries with the most oil are often lightly populated. Over the last decade, a youth "bulge" has emerged and this, combined with increased urbanization, has strained water supplies, air quality, public sanitation, and health services throughout the Muslim world. How will these young

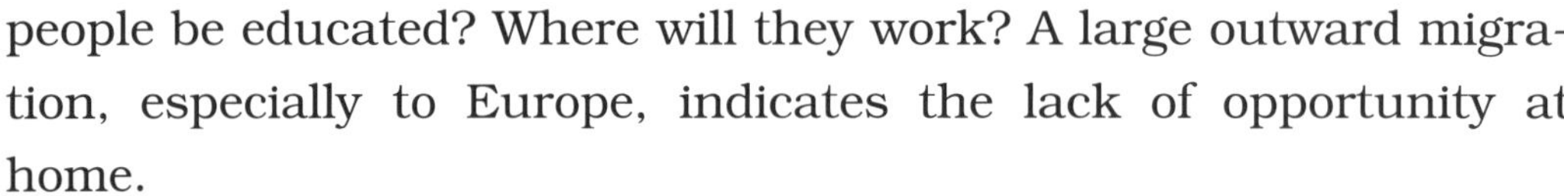

people be educated? Where will they work? A large outward migration, especially to Europe, indicates the lack of opportunity at home.

In the face of these challenges, the traditional state-dominated economic strategies have given way partly to experiments with "privatization" and foreign investment. But economic progress has come slowly, if at all, and most people have yet to benefit from "globalization," although there are pockets of prosperity, high technology (notably in Israel), and valuable natural resources (oil, gas, and minerals). Rising expectations have yet to be met.

A third important observation is the role of religion in the Middle East. Americans, who take separation of church and state for granted, should know that most countries in the region either proclaim their countries to be Muslim or allow a very large role for that religion in public life. (Islamic law, Sharia, permits people to practice Judaism and Christianity in Muslim states but only as *dhimmi*, "protected" but second-class citizens.) Among those with predominantly Muslim populations, Turkey alone describes itself as secular and prohibits avowedly religious parties in the political system. Lebanon was a Christian-dominated state, and Israel continues to be a Jewish state. Even where politics are secular, religion plays an enormous role in culture, daily life, and legislation.

Islam has deeply affected every state and people in these regions. But Islamic practices and groups vary from the well-known Sunni and Shiite groups to energetic Salafi (Wahhabi) and Sufi movements. Over the last 20 years especially, South and Central Asia have become battlegrounds for competing Shiite (Iranian) and Wahhabi (Saudi) doctrines, well financed from abroad and aggressively antagonistic toward non-Muslims and each other. Resistance to the Soviet war in Afghanistan brought these groups battle-tested warriors and organizers responsive to the doctrines made popular by Osama bin Laden and others. This newly significant struggle within Islam, superimposed on an older Muslim history, will shape political and economic destinies throughout the region and beyond.

We hope that these books will enlighten both teacher and student about the critical "hot spots" of the Muslim world. These countries would be important in their own right to Americans; arguably, after 9/11, they became vital to our national security. And the enduring impact of Islam is a crucial factor we must understand. We at the Foreign Policy Research Institute hope these books will illuminate both the facts and the prospects.

The Jordan River, which separates the Hashemite Kingdom of Jordan from Israel, has symbolic significance to both Christians and Jews. Even though Jordan is a small country with few natural resources, its location near the birthplaces of three major religions has throughout history made the region the focus of important events.

# Place in the World

Although its boundaries were drawn only in the 20th century, Jordan—officially called the ***Hashemite*** Kingdom of Jordan—is an ancient land. Despite the fact that it is mostly desert, archaeologists have discovered within its borders evidence of some of the earliest farming communities in the world. Throughout history, the land that is now the nation of Jordan existed on the fringes of various empires. Its value largely lay in its location. A number of caravan trails, originating in the Arabian Peninsula, crossed the land to reach destinations in Syria. During the era of the Ottoman Empire, pilgrims made their way through Jordan from Damascus, a major starting point for the ***hajj***, the pilgrimage to Mecca. Amman, now the capital of Jordan, was important as a meeting point for caravan trails from ancient times. But as trade routes shifted and empires came and left, towns became villages and villages disappeared under the sands of the desert.

Jordan's current cities have no old quarters, no ancient marketplaces; unlike surrounding lands, Jordan never hosted an urban area that flourished continuously for a long period. The Islamic culture that dominated this region for more than 1,000 years was linked by cities, but Jordan had none of particular importance. When the European countries turned their imperial gaze to the Middle East in the 19th century, they overlooked the Jordan region. There seemed to be no reason for colonial powers to establish themselves in this territory.

### DIVIDED PEOPLE

The people of Jordan were not, historically, a united population. Before the 20th century, the scattered villagers and tribesmen of northern Jordan considered themselves part of Greater Syria; the tribal people of southern Jordan considered themselves part of the ***Hejaz*** (spelled "Al-Hijaz" in Arabic), now part of western Saudi Arabia; and people in the villages and towns of western Jordan considered themselves part of Palestine (roughly the area of modern-day Israel and the West Bank). From the seventh century on, these groups were all largely Muslim, but each group was distinct.

The differences among the people of Jordan were not only geographical but also had to do with the ancient distinction between ***nomadic*** and settled peoples. Before the 20th century, the land of Jordan was inhabited by different groups of non-urban people who used the land and its resources in a variety of ways. There were nomadic herders, semi-nomadic groups, and settled cultivators. The settled cultivators and nomadic herdsmen needed each other. Nomads tended to be stronger in this relationship. Nomads believed their culture was more noble, free, and honorable than that of settled peoples.

These people, both settled and nomadic, lived in tribes, kinship groups who believed they were descended from a common ancestor.

Although the tribes had leaders, called ***sheikhs***, these people were fiercely independent and developed a culture that had little use for formal government. While empires came and went, little changed in the day-to-day life of the people of this region for more than 1,000 years, until the 20th century. However, the modern history of Jordan is all about change—which came quickly and uninvited by the people of the region.

## THE CREATION OF MODERN JORDAN

The forces that created modern Jordan had their origins outside its borders, with World War I and the idea of nationalism. In the Middle East, this modern idea motivated Sharif Hussein of Mecca—encouraged by the British—to start the Arab Revolt against the Ottoman Empire in 1916. His goal was to become the leader of a united Arab nation. His son Abdullah became the first ruler of modern Jordan. Like his father, Abdullah envisioned himself as the leader of a united Arab nation. During his reign he sought to unify Jordan, Syria, and Iraq. While Abdullah founded the country, credit for the modern culture of Jordan must go to his grandson, Hussein, who ruled Jordan for 46 years, until his death in 1999.

According to his family, King Hussein was part of the 42nd generation of descent from the founder of Islam, the prophet Muhammad. His tribe, the Querysh, was the most powerful tribe in the Hejaz region, whose spiritual center was Mecca. Within the tribe, Muhammad's clan was the Hashemites, who took over Mecca in the 11th century and became responsible for its religious shrines. The Hashemites lost power in 1924, when the Saud family claimed the Hejaz region for Saudi Arabia, but the Hashemite dynasty took root in Jordan and Iraq.

Hussein had a pivotal role in shaping modern Jordan. His diplomatic skills, developed throughout his long reign, were important in navigating conflicts both domestic and regional. It took many years

A portrait of the Royal Family: King Abdullah and Queen Rania are pictured here with their children, from left to right: Princess Eman, Prince Hashem, Princess Salma, and Prince Hussein. This picture, taken in Amman, was the family's New Year card of 2007.

for Hussein to establish Jordan's role amid the chaotic politics of the countries in this region. Reliance on the West gave Jordan a weak position in Middle Eastern politics. But with few natural resources to support its economy, Jordan depended on foreign aid. This aid has come largely from Western nations that see Jordan as a key player in resolving the Arab-Israeli conflict. However, by the 1980s, King Hussein's moderate voice began to be widely respected in developing foreign policy in the region.

Domestically, Hussein's greatest challenge was balancing the interests of the more cosmopolitan Palestinians among Jordan's citizens and the interests of the more traditional ***Transjordanians***, especially those from ***Bedouin*** tribes. The Bedouin formed the heart of Hashemite support in the early years of Jordan's statehood, and before 1948, tribal culture dominated the region. But in the wake of the Arab-Israeli conflict, Jordan absorbed a large Palestinian population, refugees from the formation of the country of Israel.

For many years, the violence and insecurity of the Arab-Israeli conflict spilled over into Jordan. This meant that Jordanians lived with fewer democratic privileges for the sake of national security. But in 1989 King Hussein's government allowed elections, and the country moved closer toward Hussein's goal of a modern democratic state governed by a constitutional monarchy.

Upon Hussein's death in 1999, his son Abdullah took power. Economic issues have been a major concern for King Abdullah, as the unemployment rate and the amount of foreign debt were very high. The focus of the early years of Abdullah's reign has been to aggressively address these economic issues and to continue his father's domestic and international policies. Under his leadership, Jordan has taken certain steps toward democracy, balancing the need for the support of the Arab world with ties to the West.

Although the Dead Sea looks beautiful in this photograph of its western shore, the large body of water is inhospitable because of its high salt content. Much of Jordan's land area is sandy desert.

# The Land

A land of few natural resources, the region of Jordan has nevertheless had strategic importance for thousands of years. Today, Jordan is situated between four powerful countries in the Middle East: Israel to the west, Syria to the north, Iraq to the east, and Saudi Arabia to the south. In the past, this area served as a corridor between northern and southern Arab regions. It was a buffer zone between empires in ancient times, and some would say it still serves this purpose, distancing Israel from more hostile Arab regimes to the east, most notably Iraq.

Unlike the countries that surround it, Jordan was never the center of an empire. It never supported a large population or a great urban center. Instead, Jordan existed at the margins of empires. The land and climate of Jordan shaped this identity. Less than 10 percent of the land in Jordan is suitable for growing crops; the rest is desert or steppe, which can be suitable for periodic grazing but not for farming. Only the region near the ***East Bank*** tributaries of the Jordan River receives enough rainfall for crops.

### THE JORDAN RIVER VALLEY

This region, the Jordan River Valley, forms 6 percent of Jordan's land. It is part of the Great Rift Valley, the largest fault system on the planet. Called the Al Ghawr, which means "sunken land" in Arabic, this rift is 3,000 miles (4,828 kilometers) in length, extending from southwestern Syria to Mozambique in Africa. It is still expanding at a rate of 0.04 inches (0.1 centimeters) per year, pushing the Arabian Peninsula away from Africa. In Jordan, the Al Ghawr is about 14 miles (22 km) across.

Since about 8000 B.C., the Jordan River Valley has been the home of farmers. No great ancient cities developed here because of the intense heat in the summers. However, unlike the desert regions nearby, this area has rich soil and a reliable source of water, as it is irrigated by the Jordan River. This is very important because the average yearly rainfall is only 12 inches (30 cm). Even so, the Jordan River Valley has an ideal climate for cultivating

Farms in the Jordan River Valley. Less than 10 percent of Jordan's land is suitable for farming, so only a small number of the people are involved in agriculture. Wheat, barley, citrus fruits, tomatoes, melons, and olives are among the major crops, and sheep, goats, and poultry are also raised in some areas.

A map showing Jordan's major geographic features. Much of Jordan's territory is desert, particularly in the east.

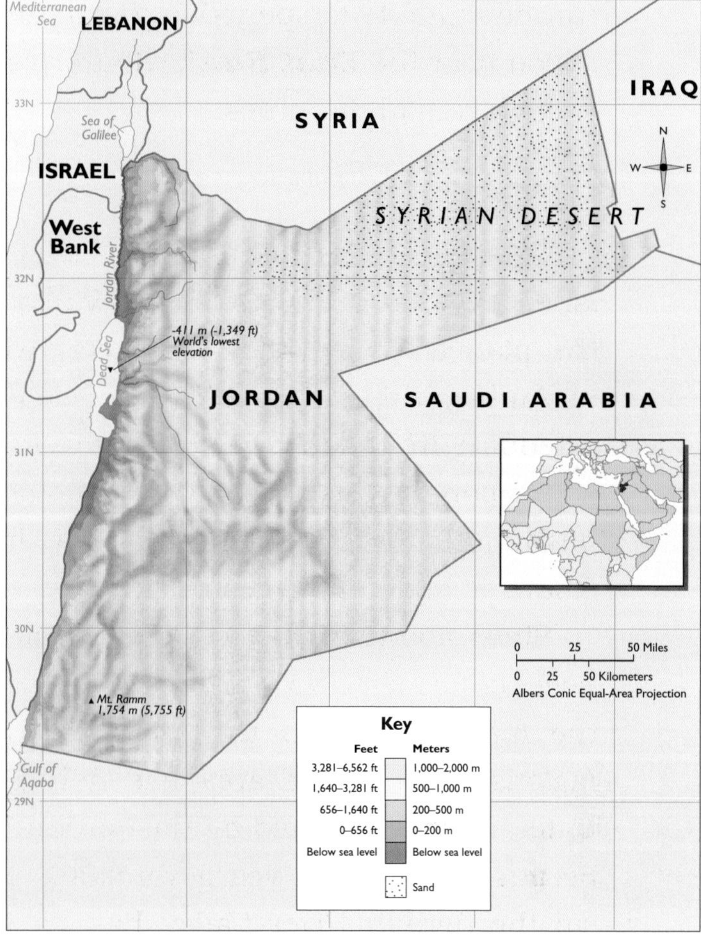


crops, with hot, dry summers and short, mild winters. In addition, the heat in this region is humid because there is a hothouse effect, caused by the steep escarpment, or cliff face, that borders the region on both the east and west. Humidity is good for certain crops.

### THE HIGHLANDS

Between the Al Ghawr in the west and the desert in the east of Jordan is the region known as the highlands, a narrow strip of high ***plateau*** that makes up about 14 percent of Jordan's land. The highlands begin in the north, near the Yarmuk River, a ***tributary*** of the Jordan River, and come to an end in the south, near the Gulf of Aqaba. Jordan's only natural forests exist in this region, where evergreen, oak, and olive trees grow wild. Since 1948, under a government forestation program, farmers have been given seedlings for free, and the areas of green in Jordan have expanded.

Wadi Arabia in southern Jordan supports only a sparse settlement of herdsmen. Wadis are dry riverbeds that fill with water after a heavy rainfall.

The highlands are cooler than the Al Ghawr region, with temperatures ranging from below freezing to about 86°F (30°C). Rainfall can vary from 2 to 13 inches (5 to 33 cm) per year, mostly between November and May. In the dry season in the summer, hot, dry winds can cause sandstorms. Frost is common in winter, and sometimes it even snows in Amman. Because of the climate, many crops are grown here; historically, the highlands were a grain-producing area.

Broken up into valleys and gorges, the highlands have three distinct regions: the northernmost is between the Yarmuk and Zarqa

Rivers. This is an area of long-settled villages and includes the city of Irbid. Farther south is the region of al-Balqa, defined by the Zarqa River in the north and, in the south, by the canyon called Wadi-al-Mujib, which runs into the Dead Sea. This area includes the city of Amman and the major towns of Az Zarqa and As Salt. Farthest south is the Bilad al-Sharat, a range of higher hills. Jabal Ram, the highest point in Jordan at 5,688 feet (1,734 meters), is found in this region. Continuing south beyond the borders of Jordan, the highlands spread into Saudi Arabia, into the region known as the Hejaz, making the populated area of Jordan a connector between Syria and the Arabian Peninsula.

South of the Jordan River Valley, the Al Ghawr runs through the Dead Sea, then through the region around the famous ruins of Petra, and finally to the Gulf of Aqaba. In this southern region, the land is marked by systems of canyons, or ***wadis***, that surround the narrow strip of highlands east of the Al Ghawr and spread into the southern desert. About 30 miles (48 km) to the east of the port of Aqaba lies the Wadi Rum, a spectacularly beautiful region where the film *Lawrence of Arabia* was set. Here, King Abdullah organized the Bedouin troops that helped him drive the Ottomans from the country in 1916.

Average summer temperatures in the Dead Sea area reach about 100°F (38°C); the hottest temperature ever recorded in Jordan was 124°F (51°C), in the Dead Sea region. In Aqaba, year-round temperatures range from 60°F to 90°F (16°C to 32°C).

### THE DESERT

East of the highlands lies the desert. About 80 percent of Jordan's area is desert, which receives less than 2 inches (5 cm) of rainfall per year. In the northern regions, the desert is made up of volcanic rock, carved by the winds for centuries. This area is called the Black Desert, but the Bedouin people know it as *bilad ash shayton*, "land of the devil." Fields of sharp, rough black lava rock, volcanic mountains, and smaller cinder cones are features of this region. The southern desert is made up of wind-eroded granite and sandstone. This region is part of the great Syro-Arabian Desert, which covers most of Syria, Jordan, Iraq, and part of northwestern Saudi Arabia. Ma'an, in the south, is the only major city in the desert region. Historically, the only residents of the desert have been Bedouin herders. The only major oasis in this region is Al-Azraq, which is in the desert east of Amman.

The desert has extreme temperatures. Winter temperatures dip below freezing at night; daytime summer temperatures may soar above 100°F (38°C).

### Water Resources

Jordan is completely landlocked except for a short strip of coastline on the northern point of the Red Sea. This beautiful coastal region, which is about 17 miles (26 km) long, faces the Gulf of Aqaba and is surrounded by a semicircle of mountains. The small city of Aqaba is the only port in Jordan, and its sunny climate draws many tourists each year.

Water, or the lack of water, has always been a defining issue in the existence of Jordan. In the highlands and the Jordan River Valley, a combination of irrigation and rainfall has made human existence possible throughout history. The most important sources of fresh water are the three major rivers: the Zarqa, the Yarmuk, and the Jordan. In northern Jordan, water from the Yarmuk and Zarqa Rivers irrigates highland crops. Farther south and west, the Jordan River irrigates the rich farming country of the Jordan River Valley.

Although the Zarqa River has its headwaters in Jordan's highlands, the other rivers begin in Syria. Thus their waters—a precious resource in the dry region—must be shared. The Yarmuk, a major

## The Geography of Jordan

**Location:** Middle East, northwest of Saudi Arabia
**Area:** about the size of Indiana
total: 35,637 square miles (92,300 sq km)
land: 35,510 square miles (91,971 sq km)
water: 127 square miles (329 sq km)
**Borders:** Iraq, 112 miles (181 km); Israel, 148 miles (238 km); Saudi Arabia, 452 miles (728 km); Syria, 233 miles (375 km); West Bank, 60 miles (97 km)
**Climate:** mostly desert; rainy season in west runs from November to April
**Terrain:** mostly desert plateau in east, highland area in west; Great Rift Valley separates East and West Banks of the Jordan River
**Elevation extremes:**
lowest point: Dead Sea—1,338 feet (408 meters) below sea level
highest point: Jabal Ram (Mt. Ramm)—5,688 feet (1,734 meters)
**Natural hazards:** droughts, sandstorms

Source: Adapted from CIA World Factbook, 2008.

tributary of the Jordan River, forms the border between Jordan and Syria for 25 miles (40 km). The Jordan River forms the border between Israel and Jordan for an equal distance. The government of Jordan has had to negotiate serious disputes with Syria and Israel over the distribution of water resources. Cooperation between these countries has allowed several dams to be built along these river systems, but water shortages are common in all three countries. Every year, both Israel and Jordan tap all of their usable water resources.

The other significant bodies of water in Jordan are the Red Sea and the Dead Sea. Both are composed of salt water, however, making them useless as sources of drinking or irrigation water without ***desalinization***. Despite its name, the Dead Sea is actually a lake.

It measures about 51 miles (82 km) long and 11 miles (18 km) wide and contains the lowest point on earth. Jordan and Israel share this unique body of water, with the international boundary running down the middle from north to south. Although the Dead Sea is fed fresh water from the Jordan River, it has no outlet, and the area's hot, dry climate produces a high rate of evaporation. Because of this, the concentration of salt in the water is extremely high—seven times higher than in ocean water. Only a few microscopic organisms can survive in these conditions—hence the Dead Sea's name. Working with Israel, however, Jordan is developing desalinization projects so that the two countries can use the waters of the Dead Sea for irrigation.

The only other important source of water in Jordan is found in the Azraq Oasis. An oasis forms wherever a reliable source of water exists in the desert. In most cases, an underground aquifer supplies the water, which can create a small spring or, as with Azraq, a large lake and wetland region. Azraq is not the only oasis in Jordan; the desert is dotted with numerous small springs and seasonal oases that support palm trees and some thorny plants. But Azraq boasts the only permanent body of water in the desert of eastern Jordan.

(Left) An ibex eats green leaves in a nature park. In recent years, the Jordanian government has taken steps to protect desert animals. (Opposite) A camel caravan passes through the Wadi Rum Desert. Camels were domesticated thousands of years ago by the Arabs, and they soon became a primary source of transport for desert-dwellers. Camels can go five to seven days without food or water and can carry loads of more than 900 pounds (336 kilograms).

### WILDLIFE

Because of its environmental significance, the modern government of Jordan has turned the region near Azraq into a wildlife preserve. The desert creatures that seek out the waters of Azraq include wild grazing animals that have been hunted for millennia, such as the Arabian oryx, gazelle, and ibex. Today, environmental laws protect all of these creatures from hunting. Other animals that live near the oases in this desert region include the hyena, ostrich, mongoose, sand adder, and more than 300 species of birds.

Wildlife in Jordan is restricted to the desert as a result of thousands of years of human settlement in the highlands and fertile regions. Agricultural fields and grazing herds have limited the resources available to other animals. Sheep and goats continue to be the most important herd animals. Since cars and highways have taken over the transport of goods across the desert, camels no longer constitute a significant animal population. Today, Jordan's few camels are raised by the even smaller numbers of remaining semi-nomadic Bedouins.

The Roman ruins of Jerash, north of Amman, are surrounded by more modern neighborhoods. The Romans controlled the area that today is Jordan from about A.D. 106 until the fourth century. Jordan has been on the fringes of great empires and civilizations throughout history.

# History

Human settlement in the area that today makes up Jordan is believed to date to around 8000 B.C. The Jordan River Valley is among the first places wheat was cultivated, which made possible the growth of permanent communities.

By 2000 B.C., this region was home to many tribal peoples, including the Israelites, Amorites, Canaanites, Ammonites, Moabites, Edomites, and Arameans, who were often at war with one another. Around 965 B.C., King David, a powerful Israelite leader, pushed his armies into the land on the East Bank of the Jordan River. The next 200 years were marked by conflict between the Israelites and other tribal kingdoms of the area. After the eighth century B.C., a series of powerful empires conquered the region, but none fully established their culture there. One after the other, Assyrians, Babylonians, Persians, and Greeks all claimed this territory before yielding to another, more powerful, empire. By the third century B.C., the area that is now Jordan was dominated by the culture of the Greeks, Jews, and Nabateans.

### Nabateans, Romans, Byzantines, and Sassanians

One of the few ancient cultures that originated in the land of Jordan, the Nabateans ruled parts of southern Jordan and Palestine for about 1,000 years. A people of Arab origin, the Nabateans built the city of Petra, carving the faces of buildings into the sandstone walls of the wadis in which they made their homes. Petra was a major stopping point on the caravan route from Arabia to the Mediterranean. The Nabateans were mainly spice merchants, and they traded with the Jews, Persians, and early Greeks. With sophisticated water technology, they built a secret system of cisterns to store water from rain and snowmelt. In A.D. 106, the Roman Empire annexed the Nabatean Kingdom.

Rome's control of the region weakened after the year 300, and trade and trade centers declined. Nomadic life in this region increased as village populations decreased. Even the roads built by the Romans began to disappear because nomadic populations relied on camels instead of wheeled vehicles. The remaining towns were dominated by Christian communities, which had been established in the Jordan area largely because of Roman persecution of Christians in the first century A.D. Most rural people continued to practice traditional religions.

**Scenes from the popular movie *Indiana Jones and the Last Crusade* were filmed in Petra. The ancient city was a center of the Nabatean civilization.**

In the fourth century this region became part of the Byzantine Empire. Centered in Constantinople (the site of modern-day Istanbul, Turkey), this Greek-influenced civilization arose from the division of the Roman Empire into the Eastern

The Treasury, a monument carved from a red sandstone cliff in Petra, is the first thing a visitor sees when coming through the Siq, a canyon that leads to Petra. It is about 130 feet (40 meters) tall. Though no one is sure what its purpose was, most people believe it was the tomb of a Nabatean king.

Roman (Byzantine) and Western Roman Empires. During the Byzantine era towns in what is today western Jordan saw a great deal of construction. But the area was also wracked by turmoil as the Byzantines vied for control with the rival Sassanian Empire, centered in Persia. Both empires coveted the lucrative East-West trade routes that ran through modern-day Jordan, Syria, and Israel. In the early seventh century the Sassanians managed to conquer and occupy this area, but after 15 years the Byzantine Empire regained control, in 629.

Neither empire paid attention to developments farther south in the vast deserts of the Arabian Peninsula. But within a few years, Arab tribes—unified under a new religion—would sweep out of the peninsula and begin a series of remarkable conquests that forever altered the political, social, and religious landscape of the region.

### THE RISE OF ISLAM

The religion that inspired the conquering Arab armies was Islam. Its beginnings date to around A.D. 610, when the prophet Muhammad, an Arab merchant living in Mecca (in modern-day Saudi Arabia), claimed to have received the first of many revelations from God. Muhammad began preaching God's message, the essence of which is that there is only one God and that believers must submit to God's will. The Arabs of the time worshiped many idols, so Muhammad was initially not well received, and in 622 he and his followers—called Muslims—fled Mecca and settled in the oasis town of Medina. After years of fighting, however, Muhammad's forces triumphed, taking Mecca and converting most of the Arabian Peninsula to Islam.

A year after the Prophet's death in 632, Arab armies fighting under the banner of Islam swept into the region of Jordan. By the end of the seventh century, most of the Arab peoples in what is now Jordan had converted to Islam, although small communities of Jews as well as Greek and Arab Christians remained. It is estimated that in the highlands of Jordan about 15 percent of the population remained Christian, including settled and nomadic peoples. These non-Muslim communities paid a poll tax and had certain legal restrictions, but they often thrived commercially.

The empires of Islam established both religious and political control over the vast regions of the Middle East that they eventually conquered. In the beginning, the leader of the Islamic empire was called a ***caliph***, and his role included guarding the traditions of the

Prophet and enforcing Islamic law. The first Islamic caliphate after the death of Muhammad was called the Omayyad Caliphate, named for the powerful clan that eventually conquered and ruled all of the Arabian Peninsula, northern Africa, and southern Europe for 100 years.

In the region of Jordan, the rule of the Omayyads didn't change everyday life much because Islamic rulers considered the area unimportant. Omayyad culture was urban, and most of the lands of Jordan remained rural or wild. Some towns in this region prospered because they were near important trade routes, and the Omayyads built palaces and hunting lodges in the countryside, but Bedouin tribes and clans ruled their own territories. Other Islamic empires rose and fell, but the Jordan region was never a significant part of their domains.

When European Christian knights launched the First Crusade and captured Jerusalem in 1099, they claimed the western region of Jordan as part of their Christian kingdom. That kingdom was fairly short-lived, however. Saladin, the ***sultan*** of Egypt, defeated the crusaders in 1187 and restored the rule of the Islamic empires. Jordan remained part of the Islamic empire based in Egypt for the next 300 years.

## THE OTTOMAN EMPIRE

In the mid-1500s, a new, more powerful Islamic empire took over this region. The Ottoman Empire was based in what is now Turkey and had conquered the lands of eastern Europe before taking control of the Jordan region. The Ottoman sultan used Islamic holy law, the ***Sharia***, as the rule of the land. The sultan imposed strict taxes but allowed for local administration of government by Arabs loyal to the Ottoman Empire.

The Ottoman Empire was divided into *vilayets* (provinces) ruled by *pashas* (governors). Modern Jordan was divided between the vilayets of Beirut and Damascus. The Ottomans named this area ***Transjordan***; once again, it was not important to the empire except as a pilgrimage route to the holy sites in Mecca and Medina. During the Ottoman period, most of the Jordan region did not grow culturally or economically, and most of the desert regions of Jordan were not under direct Ottoman control. Much of the desert and highlands remained the territory of the Bedouin tribes.

From the 17th century onward, the power of the Ottomans declined under pressure from increasingly powerful European nations. At the same time, corruption weakened the empire from within. By the 19th century, European trading corporations controlled much of the Middle Eastern economy. The Ottoman Empire responded by trying to modernize to compete with the European powers. Attempts to impose law and order and collect taxes in the Jordan region met with great tribal resistance in the mid-19th century. But the Ottomans built the Hejaz Railway, which ran from Istanbul to Medina, going through Amman in Jordan. They completed the project in 1908.

## THE ROOTS OF MODERN JORDAN

The contest between European nations and the Ottoman Empire for control of the region was definitively settled during World War I. When the hostilities broke out in 1914, the Ottomans allied themselves with Germany, whose enemies included France and Great Britain, two nations with strong interests in the Middle East. Although most Ottoman subjects remained loyal to the sultan, the Arabs of the Hejaz did not. These desert tribes, as well as those in Jordan, had never fully been under Ottoman control.

Taking advantage of the situation, Sharif Hussein bin Ali, head of the Hashemite tribe and ***emir*** of Mecca, began secret negotiations with British authorities. Hussein, a leader of the nationalist Arabs, threw his support behind Britain and its allies against the

The sultan Suleyman is considered the greatest of the Ottoman rulers. During his reign (1520–66) the Ottoman Empire was at the height of its power politically, economically, and culturally. Suleyman was known to Europeans as "the Magnificent"; Turks and Arabs knew him as "the Lawgiver" because he issued a set of laws that combined traditional Islamic *Sharia* with the legal codes of the Ottomans.

Ottomans in exchange for vague promises about the establishment of an independent Arab state after the war. Arab nationalists had long resisted the suppression of Arab culture in the Ottoman Empire and wanted a unified Arab nation. Arab nationalism became a Hashemite fight because, throughout the history of Islam, movements of protest sought out the leadership of the Hashemites, descendants of the prophet Muhammad. With the support of the British, Hussein and his sons, Abdullah and Faisal, led the Arab Revolt against the Ottomans in 1916. But after helping Britain and its allies win World War I, Hussein failed to get what he thought he had been promised.

At the end of the war in 1918, the region was in chaos, and the Arab nationalists quickly tried to gain control. In 1919, after a meeting of Syrian, Transjordanian, and Lebanese leaders, Faisal was appointed king of Syria, with his capital in Damascus. But the European powers had other plans. At the ***League of Nations*** conference in San Remo, Italy, in 1920, France was given a ***mandate***

The British soldier-adventurer Thomas Edward Lawrence (1888–1935), better known as Lawrence of Arabia, was involved in the 1916 Arab Revolt. After the First World War broke out in 1914, the British had secretly encouraged Arab nationalists to rise up against their Ottoman rulers, who had aligned themselves with Germany and Austria-Hungary. In return for the support of such Arab leaders as Sharif Hussein bin Ali, the head of the Hashemites, the British had agreed to support an independent Arab state after the war. Sharif Hussein's sons Abdullah and Faisal led the Arab forces during the Revolt, which assisted the British forces under General E. H. Allenby that defeated the Turks.

for Lebanon and Syria, and the French quickly removed Faisal from power. At the same conference, Great Britain was given a mandate for Iraq and Palestine, which it divided into Palestine and Transjordan.

In exchange for control over the region, the mandate required Britain to develop the economy and political organization of the mandated areas. But Britain had its own conflicting interests, including protecting its route to India through the Suez Canal and having access to a cheap source of oil in Iraq. In addition, British authorities had earlier committed to—and the mandate required—the creation of a Jewish homeland in Palestine.

Zionism—as the movement for a Jewish homeland was called—had developed in parallel to the early flickers of Arab nationalism. In the 1870s European Jews bought land in Palestine, hoping to set up a Jewish community as a refuge from persecution in eastern

Europe. In 1897 Theodor Herzl, a Hungarian-born Austrian writer, started the Zionist Organization, with the purpose of establishing a Jewish homeland in Palestine. Jewish settlers began arriving in the region, and by World War I, Jews made up about 12 percent of the population of Palestine.

As the postwar British mandates were being set up, Arab nationalists grew extremely wary and resentful. They had not received the anticipated large, independent Arab state. Instead, there were British- and French-ruled mandates, and the one in Palestine facilitated a Jewish national homeland. Furthermore, the borders of the proposed Jewish home were established according to biblical scholars' understanding of the ancient land of Israel, but the arrangements failed to take into account the Arabs' political aspirations for independence based on their thousand-year residence in the land. Conflict grew between organized, nationalistic Jewish settlers and native Arabs. The strife led some Palestinians to migrate into the area of Transjordan.

In the meantime, there was essentially no law and order in the Jordan region. In rural areas, village sheikhs set up their own rule, with nomadic Bedouins refusing to recognize any local authority.

## ENTER ABDULLAH

This region was considered ungovernable when Abdullah—the son of Sharif Hussein, who had led the Arab Revolt of 1916—arrived in the town of Ma'an in 1920. He planned to begin a campaign to establish an independent Arab state, which would include the territory of modern-day Syria, Jordan, and Iraq, along with the Hejaz, where his father still ruled. But Abdullah had no real power on which to base his claims. He was dependent on support from Britain.

In 1921 Britain worked out an agreement with Abdullah and his brother Faisal: Faisal would take Iraq and give up Syria in recognition of the League of Nations mandate, and Abdullah would take Transjordan, which was detached from the Palestinian mandate. Britain persuaded Abdullah to set up his seat of government in Amman, instead of Ma'an, which would lessen his claim on the Hejaz. It was also understood that Abdullah would not try to retake Syria from the French. Before he left Ma'an, however, Abdullah addressed his people in terms that demonstrated he had not abandoned his Arab nationalist vision: "I do not wish to see any among you identify yourselves by geographical region. I wish to see everyone, rather, trace his descent to the Arabian peninsula, from which we all originate. All Arab countries are the country of every Arab."

In 1922 Abdullah, in conjunction with the British, set up the borders of Transjordan. Britain gave Transjordan status as a national state preparing for independence in 1923, and Abdullah was named emir. At the same time, a combined military and police force, the Arab Legion, was started under the command of a British officer in order to establish control of the region. Made up primarily of Bedouins, the Arab Legion became, in time, the key support of Abdullah's regime.

Emir Abdullah had a difficult task before him. His small country needed to be both united and pacified in the early years. At first, Transjordan had a population of less than 400,000, only 20 percent of whom lived in towns with more than 10,000 inhabitants. The rest were villagers and pastoral nomadic and semi-nomadic people. The capital of Amman was a town, not a city. Many families had relatives on both sides of the Jordan River. During the Ottoman period, these people had not thought of themselves as Palestinians or Transjordanians. Only after World War I did they gradually begin to identify with the countries of Palestine or Transjordan.

In the early years of his reign, Abdullah worked to establish law and order in Transjordan, but this task was complicated. In the mid-1920s, conflicts in the region caused Arab nationalists to flee

With the support of Great Britain, the sons of Sharif Hussein gained control of different areas. Seated left to right in this photograph, taken November 1923 in Baghdad, are King Faisal I of Iraq, Emir Abdullah I of Transjordan, and King Ali of the Hejaz (a short-lived Arab kingdom that is now part of Saudi Arabia).

from Syria and the Hejaz into Transjordan and create problems for the new government. Raiding among Bedouin tribes and tribal unrest in the Petra area were also a problem. In 1927 an earthquake destroyed the new capital of Amman. Because Jewish funds helped to rebuild the city, Abdullah tried to work with Jewish interests across the Jordan River in Palestine. But Abdullah's willingness to work with Jews caused conflict with Palestinians within Jordan, both at this time and later.

Transjordan still was closely connected to Britain during this period. The Anglo-Transjordan Agreement of 1928 created a temporary constitution and a legislative council, a representative body whose powers were mainly advisory. Britain still exercised much control over foreign affairs, the armed forces, and state finances, but in exchange it gave Transjordan a significant amount of financial support every year. When World War II broke out, Jordan was an ally of Britain.

However, Emir Abdullah was slowly moving his country toward independence. In 1945 Abdullah participated in the formation of the League of Arab States, or Arab League, which included

Transjordan, Egypt, Syria, Lebanon, Saudi Arabia, Iraq, and Yemen. In 1946 Transjordan became politically independent, although the young nation was still reliant on Britain economically. Renaming his country Jordan, Abdullah crowned himself king and established a new constitution.

At this time, the British were ready to give up the entire mandate in the region. By 1947 the hostilities between Arabs and Jews made Palestine too expensive and difficult for Britain to oversee, and the British were confident that the Jews had enough control of the economic resources in Palestine to take care of themselves. Because of the potentially explosive impact of the British withdrawal, the recently established United Nations intervened. It decided on a plan to create separate Arab and Jewish states, with international status for Jerusalem. While the Zionists accepted the UN resolution, the Arab League was against it and vowed to prevent it from taking effect. Only Jordan voted in favor of the resolution, as Abdullah thought it was the best of a bad situation for the Palestinians.

In 1948 the Zionists declared the formation of the State of Israel in what had been Palestine, even though twice as many Palestinians as Jews lived there. The armies of the Arab League, which included Jordan, attacked Israel as promised, with King Abdullah as the commander-in-chief. During the war, hundreds of Palestinian villages were destroyed. Many villagers were killed or driven out. Large numbers fled to other Arab states, including Jordan. Because the armies of the Arab League were unable to coordinate their goals, Abdullah's Arab Legion gained control of central and east Palestine for Jordan. This area, just west of the Jordan River, is called the West Bank and included East Jerusalem. Abdullah wanted control of this area partly because he feared a Palestinian state under the control of his enemies in the Palestinian leadership, notably the Mufti Haj Amin al-Husseini. He justified his actions as a defense of Muslim holy places in Jerusalem, Bethlehem, and Hebron.

At the end of the war, in 1949, Jordan signed a truce with Israel. The agreement divided control of the West Bank between Israel and Jordan and gave Jordan the task of policing the border between the two countries. In 1950, however, Abdullah made the West Bank and its resident Palestinians part of Jordan. Britain and Pakistan were the only nations that approved of this ***annexation***. The other countries of the Arab League sharply criticized Abdullah, charging that he was suppressing the Palestinian people.

Jordan gained a great deal by expanding its territory into the West Bank, including revenue from tourism to sites considered holy by Christians, Jews, and Muslims. But the 1948 war with Israel was expensive for Jordan also. Israel refused to allow many Palestinian refugees displaced by the fighting to return to their homes. No settlements were made to deal with these refugees, as Britain and the United States assumed the Palestinians would be absorbed into the surrounding Arab states, especially Jordan. As a result, Jordan had to support many thousands of Palestinian refugees who had no place to go.

By annexing the West Bank, King Abdullah made his task of leading Jordan's people far more complicated. In 1950 the West Bank had twice as many Palestinian residents as Jordan's East Bank. It had a population of about 500,000 native residents plus up to 500,000 refugees from what is now Israel. This segment of Jordan's population was often at odds with the more traditional Transjordanians, who controlled Abdullah's government. While he wanted to respond to the concerns of the Palestinians, Abdullah also wanted to build a modern state, and he still had Arab nationalist goals.

In 1951, while traveling to Al-Aqsa Mosque in Jerusalem for Friday prayers, King Abdullah was assassinated by a Palestinian

The Middle East is the birthplace for three of the world's major religions—Judaism, Christianity, and Islam. All three religions see Jerusalem as a sacred city—to Jews, it is the holy city of God; to Christians, it is the place where Jesus Christ was crucified, was buried, and rose from the dead; to Muslims, it is the place where Muhammad made his *Miraaj* ("Night Journey") to heaven to contemplate the oneness of God. Jerusalem and other holy sites in the West Bank were part of the Hashemite Kingdom of Jordan from 1949 until 1967, when the West Bank was captured by Israel during the Six-Day War.

gunman. His 15-year-old grandson Hussein, whom the gunman also shot at, was not injured.

Crown Prince Talal, Abdullah's eldest son, assumed the throne. Under his government, a new, more democratic constitution was ratified in January 1952. But Talal suffered from schizophrenia, a serious mental illness, and as his symptoms became increasingly severe, his prime minister convinced him to abdicate his throne to seek treatment. A council of ministers ruled until 1953, when Hussein, Talal's oldest son, turned 18—the minimum age established by the new constitution for a king to be crowned.

### HUSSEIN TAKES OVER

Although the young king had been educated for leadership, he faced many problems. His country's weak economy was almost entirely dependent on foreign aid. In the early years of his reign, he also dealt with powerful prime ministers who wanted to govern Jordan themselves. Border battles flared when the ***fedayeen***, Palestinian fighters based in Jordan, launched terrorist incursions into Israel and Israel retaliated by attacking Jordanian villages near its borders.

Hussein's biggest challenge, however, was his divided population. Transjordanians, who made up the government, tended to be conservative and traditional, but Palestinians, who constituted more than half of the population, tended to be more modern. The young, educated urban Palestinians were politically sophisticated. They were interested in Arab nationalism and admired the socialist governments of their Arab neighbors. Believing the Hashemite monarchy to be an outdated institution, they looked to Egypt and its charismatic ruler, Gamal Abdel Nasser, for Arab leadership. In an effort to control the unrest in his country, King Hussein tightened security and placed limits on civic freedoms and rights.

While Hussein's government struggled to maintain control domestically, it was also trying to stake out its place internationally and foster relationships with other Arab countries. In 1955 Jordan joined the United Nations. In 1956, responding to anti-Western criticism, King Hussein ended British control of the Arab Legion and decided not to join the pro-Western Baghdad Pact. Instead, he encouraged the creation of the Arab Solidarity Agreement, by which Jordan was supposed to receive funds from

Saudi Arabia and Egypt, thus eliminating the need for British support. Because the funds did not come through as promised, Hussein sought and received help from the United States in 1957, based on Jordan's status as a country resisting communism.

At the time, the United States and the communist Soviet Union were engaged in a struggle for global power known as the Cold War. This struggle, which emerged in the wake of World War II, never exploded into a direct military confrontation between the two superpowers. Rather, the United States and the Soviet Union attempted to thwart each other's designs by enlisting like-minded allies around the world. Nevertheless, allies of the competing superpowers—with the support of their patrons—sometimes went to war, often with great loss of life.

Powerful Arab nations such as Syria and Egypt proclaimed that the Arab world should remain neutral in the struggle between the Soviet Union and the United States (though their behavior sometimes failed to match their public pronouncements). It was difficult for Jordan to overcome its economic dependence on the United States, however. Unlike other Arab nations, Jordan had no oil, few other natural resources, and little of value except its strategic location. Nevertheless, Hussein's overtures toward the United States caused tensions between Jordan and other Arab nations. Domestically his position was somewhat shaky as well. After a failed attempt to overthrow the government by military officers inspired by Egypt's leader Gamal Abdel Nasser, political activity was outlawed, and Jordan moved away from its path toward democracy. In spite of the heightened security, Hussein was the target of several assassination attempts between 1959 and 1961.

During the 1960s Jordan's economy began to improve. U.S. and British investment in the development of mining interests and oil refining began to add to the economy. Also, many educated Jordanians, especially Palestinian-Jordanians, found work in the

King Hussein I with his second wife, Princess Muna (the mother of Jordan's current king), in a 1962 photograph. Hussein ascended to the throne when he turned 18 in 1953, after the assassination of his grandfather and the abdication of his father.

oil industry in the Persian Gulf states, and their ***remittances*** (the money they sent home to their families) bolstered the economy. Overall, this period saw growth in the Jordanian middle class.

### THE PALESTINIAN PROBLEM

In 1964 the nations of the Arab League formed the Palestine Liberation Organization (PLO), whose purpose was to coordinate the activities of Palestinian groups seeking to destroy Israel. Over the next two decades, the PLO would present enormous pitfalls for King Hussein. Palestinian guerrillas used Jordan as a base from which to attack Israel, provoking Israeli counterstrikes on Jordanian villages. In addition, the PLO tried to tax West Bank citizens and distribute arms to villagers and refugees. Hussein's efforts to rein in the PLO heightened tensions between the king and the hundreds of thousands of Palestinians in his nation. These tensions, in turn, may have contributed to what many historians consider Hussein's biggest mistake.

In 1967 Egypt, along with Iraq, Syria, and Jordan, mobilized to attack Israel. The Israelis launched preemptive strikes on June 5, destroying the Arab air forces and igniting what came to be known as the Six-Day War. Despite Israeli requests that he stay out of the fighting, King Hussein, misled by false Egyptian reports, joined in the war. The result was disastrous. After just three days of fighting, Israeli forces had smashed the Jordanians, taking the West Bank and East Jerusalem from Jordan. Jordan lost up to 6,000 troops, and about 224,000 refugees fled the West Bank to Jordan's East Bank. The Jordanian tourist economy would also suffer a heavy blow, as Jordan no longer contained the Holy Land.

The war ended without a peace agreement. In November 1967 the United Nations offered Resolution 242, which had four key points: Israel must withdraw from territories taken in war to "secure and recognized borders"; there must be an end of hostilities; there must be an acknowledgment of the sovereignty of all states, including Israel; and there must be a fair resolution to the refugee problem.

Israeli tanks advance during the Six-Day War, 1967. By June 10, when the fighting was halted, Israel controlled all Jordanian territory west of the Jordan River, as well as the Sinai Peninsula and the Golan Heights.

In the aftermath of the Six-Day War, Yasir Arafat gained control of the PLO. Arafat, an Egyptian-born Palestinian, was the leader of a militant faction called Fatah. Although King Hussein advocated Resolution 242, Arafat refused to comply with it, on the grounds that the resolution would recognize Israel. Meanwhile, the PLO—with aid from other Arab countries—grew into a virtual state-within-a-state inside Jordan. Arafat's organization, King Hussein believed, threatened to destabilize his government—and not just because of its airplane hijackings or guerrilla incursions into Israel. By 1970 members of the PLO were speaking rather openly of overthrowing Jordan's king. In September of that year Hussein took action, ordering his army to expel the PLO from Jordan. In a brief but bitter fight, the Jordanian army routed the PLO forces, killing thousands. Arafat would eventually leave Jordan and reestablish his organization in Beirut, Lebanon.

In Jordan in the aftermath of the fighting, law and order was maintained by the very strong presence of the secret police—called the Dairat al Mukhabarat, or General Intelligence Department—and a suspension of many constitutional rights and freedoms under martial law. For many years, this force focused on getting rid of Palestinian militant groups and illegal political organizations. Its tactics, which included arrest, torture, and even murder, were often criticized by human rights groups.

Although Hussein had removed the immediate threat posed by Yasir Arafat and the PLO, critical issues remained. Who should represent the interests of the Palestinian people? What was the place of Palestinian refugees in Jordanian society? Of all the Arab states that harbored refugees, Jordan had done the most to integrate the Palestinians into its population, granting them voting rights and citizenship. But such rights came at the cost of their identity as a separate people, and many Palestinians wanted to determine their own destiny.

The king would not go to war with Israel again. He sat out the October 1973 Yom Kippur War—at some cost to his relations with the other Arab states. In 1974, at the Rabat Summit, the PLO was recognized by Arab nations as representing the Palestinian people. Only Jordan protested.

### Changes and Challenges

Despite the problems with the PLO, in the late 1970s Jordan began to advance its position as an independent nation in the Middle East. In 1976, when the U.S. government refused to sell arms to Jordan, Hussein began to distance himself from the West, a stance that improved relations with his Arab neighbors. When President Anwar el-Sadat of Egypt signed the Camp David Accords, a peace agreement with Israel, in 1978, Hussein joined the other Arab states in cutting off ties with Egypt. And as some Israeli leaders began to push the idea that land in Jordan, not the West Bank, should be used for a Palestinian state, the Palestinian relationship to Jordan became less hostile.

In the 1980s King Hussein slowly emerged as a respected Arab leader. He balanced economic ties to the West with Arab concerns, and official opposition to Israel with a carefully cultivated secret relationship with various Israeli leaders. In 1983 Hussein was openly critical of the United States for its inability to pressure Israel to stop Jewish settlements in the West Bank. In 1984 Jordan became the first Arab country to reestablish diplomatic relations with Egypt.

This new strength gave Hussein an opportunity to improve the domestic situation. In response to agitation for more public participation in the political process, Hussein convened a special meeting of Jordan's legislative branch to prepare for elections. In 1984 a new electoral law was passed, recognizing the different constituencies within Jordan: Arabs, Christians, Palestinians (including those in refugee camps), and Circassians and Chechens (Russian groups who settled in Jordan in the 19th century). However, because this political reform included the West Bank as part of the state of Jordan, relations between Hussein and the PLO grew tense again, and the elections were postponed.

In December 1987 the ***intifada***, or Palestinian uprising, began in the West Bank, with young Palestinians fighting the Israeli army in the streets. Hussein finally realized that he could not exert either control or influence there. In 1988 the king gave up Jordan's claim to the West Bank. By letting go, Hussein could finally work on moving his country toward a modern democracy. In 1989 Hussein announced the establishment of a new National Assembly, to be elected by the citizens of Jordan. After the elections in November 1989, Jordan had a new 80-person Assembly and a national charter that established full equality of citizenship for all Jordanians.

Just as Jordan had a chance to prosper in its newfound security, the Middle East was enveloped in another crisis. In 1990 Iraq, a crucial Jordanian trading partner and supplier of its oil, seized Kuwait. The United States quickly organized an international coalition to force Iraq out. King Hussein avoided both the Gulf War and a potential civil war by remaining neutral, advocating diplomacy but not allowing Saddam Hussein to use Jordan to attack Israel. With this independent stance the king won the approval of his own people—including his Palestinian subjects—and of Israelis at the same time.

Still, the king's stance was costly. Jordan lost economic aid from both Western countries and Arab states. The war caused further hardship because Jordan was flooded with refugees from Kuwait and Iraq, including many Palestinian workers.

After the war, strong ties were quickly reestablished with the United States. Aid that Jordan counted on to keep its economy going resumed.

In his last decade of leadership in Jordan, Hussein gained the confidence of his citizens, the respect of his Arab neighbors, and Israeli support. At the Arab-Israeli peace talks in Madrid in 1992, Jordan was a key player, making it possible for the Palestinian delegation to participate. In October 1994, Jordan recognized the State of Israel, and Hussein signed a formal peace treaty with Israel.

With Jordan enjoying peaceful relations with its neighbors and domestic tranquility, the focus of Hussein's last years as king was on the economic health of his country. In the 1990s foreign debt was a concern, so Jordan passed laws encouraging domestic investment. In 1995 Jordan reached new agreements with its lenders in the International Monetary Fund, giving the country better terms for the repayment of its foreign debt. Hussein also hosted a Middle East and North African economic summit to discuss the issues of economic growth facing countries like Jordan.

In 1999 King Hussein died of lymphatic cancer. He had ruled Jordan for 46 years, the longest-ruling leader of the Middle East. Just before his death, he named his eldest son, Abdullah, as crown prince. In spite of some concerns about the transition of power, Abdullah assumed the throne without much drama.

## King Abdullah

In the early years of his reign, King Abdullah focused on continuing his father's efforts to foster peace in the Middle East and to develop the economy of Jordan. When Abdullah assumed the throne, foreign debt stood at $8.4 billion and unemployment was close to 20 percent. He appointed an economist, Ali Abu Raghab, as his prime minister, and focused on getting private companies to invest in the Jordanian mining industry and telecommunications firms. Because of progress made in creating an investment climate in Jordan, Abdullah signed a free trade agreement with the United States in 2000, giving Jordan unrestricted access to U.S. markets.

Abdullah II is crowned in Amman on February 8, 1999, a day after the death of his father, King Hussein. Hussein, whose portrait appears to his son's left, chose Abdullah as his successor just two weeks before dying of cancer. As king, Abdullah is considered head of the Hashemite family, which is descended from the prophet Muhammad and has played a significant role in the region for nearly 2,000 years.

That same year, Jordan joined the World Trade Organization.

Abdullah has done well in the recent years to help bring his country to a more stable economic footing. Yet there continues to be minor problems with inflation, and unemployment rates remain high. One of the biggest obstacles has been the instability in the region, flowing from the U.S. invasion of Iraq. Iraq had been one of Jordan's most consistent oil suppliers and trade partners, and its instability forced Abdullah to look to other countries in the Middle East for resources. The war also led to a huge influx of refugees into Jordan, which has burdened the country in many ways. Going forward, the king has mentioned trying to make Jordan a democracy one day.

الاجتماع التحضيري لوزراء الخارجية العرب
لمجلس الجامعة العربية على مستوى القمة

A group of foreign ministers from 22 Arab countries meets in Amman. Jordan is considered one of the most democratic countries in the Arab world. The country is a constitutional monarchy; laws are made by an elected parliament and the king is the chief executive, responsible for carrying them out.

# The Economy, Politics, and Religion

When Britain drew the boundaries of Transjordan in 1921, its motives involved strategic self-interest; creating a country with a vital economy was not a priority. Less than 10 percent of the land in Transjordan was arable, and it had few natural resources. Its tribal people lacked a strong agricultural tradition, and it had no major cities as economic centers. Because of these factors, Jordan's economy was, for many years, dependent on external sources. Despite its reliance on foreign aid, especially from Britain and the United States, and setbacks, such as the loss of the West Bank in 1967, the Jordanian economy has grown slowly, bringing the country toward financial independence.

King Hussein did much during the last decade of his reign to confront the biggest problems facing Jordan's economy, including a large trade deficit, national debt, the cost of supporting Palestinian refugees, and a high unemployment rate. Following the direction set by his father, King Abdullah has worked to take advantage of Jordan's strengths, such as its strategic geographic location, educated workforce, and free enterprise economy.

### ECONOMIC OVERVIEW

Jordan, a small nation of around 6 million people, also has a small economy. Its ***gross domestic product (GDP)***—the total value of goods and services produced within the country in a one-year period—stood at $16.01 billion in 2008. In total size, Jordan ranked 98th among the world's economies, according to the International Money Fund.

By various measures of individual wealth, the average Jordanian is poor by Western standards but in the lower middle-income range worldwide. Adjusting for differences in the local cost of living, per capita income in Jordan was estimated at $4,700 in 2007. Poverty is a significant and chronic problem, however. Recent estimates of the proportion of Jordanians living below the poverty line range from about 10 percent to 15, but could be as high as 30 percent.

Jordan has faced many economic hurdles over the last several decades. Dependence on foreign aid, and debt, are two interrelated issues. Lacking significant natural resources, Jordan has historically depended on foreign aid. Since the mid-1970s, most of that aid has come from the Organization of Arab Petroleum Exporting Countries (OAPEC), particularly Saudi Arabia. A worldwide economic recession in the 1980s made it harder for the OAPEC countries to continue to help Jordan, however. As aid declined, Jordan began to borrow heavily from foreign sources. In turn, Jordan's economy was seriously disrupted by the Gulf War of 1991, making it difficult for the country to service its debt.

Another problem that continues to plague Jordan is the lack of foreign investment. In most capitalist economies individual companies buy and sell products, driving the economy. But in Jordan, the government is the major customer and employer, regulating the spending and investing. Because of the instability of the region surrounding Jordan, the government has had difficulty attracting foreign investors and also has been forced to spend a great deal on defense. While the government's control of the economy also deters foreign investors, King Abdullah has taken steps to encourage investment by Jordanian businesses and replace government-owned concerns with private industry.

Jordan's major trade partners include Arab neighbors such as Iraq, Saudi Arabia, Lebanon, Kuwait, and Syria, along with Germany, the United Kingdom, Italy, the United States, Japan,

## The Economy of Jordan

**Gross domestic product (GDP*):** $16.01 billion
**Per capita income:** $4,700 (purchasing power parity)
**Inflation:** 5.4%
**Natural resources:** phosphates, potash
**Agriculture (3.5% of GDP):** wheat, barley, citrus, tomatoes, melons, olives; sheep, goats, poultry (2007 est.)
**Industry (10.3% of GDP):** phosphate mining, petroleum refining, cement, potash, fertilizers, paper and cardboard, light manufacturing (2007 est.)
**Services (86.2% of GDP):** government services, banking, insurance, consulting, tourism (2007 est.)
**Foreign trade:**
Imports—$12.02 billion: crude oil, food, livestock, manufacturing and transport equipment, consumer goods.
Exports—$5.7 billion: chemicals, phosphates, fertilizers, manufactured goods (such as machinery).
**Currency exchange rate:** 0.7078 Jordanian dinars = U.S. $1 (2002)

*GDP, or gross domestic product, is the total value of goods and services produced in a country annually.
All figures are 2008 estimates unless otherwise noted. Sources: World Bank; CIA World Factbook, 2008.

A technician prepares a document for printing at National Press in Amman. In recent years many companies in Jordan have modernized by upgrading to the latest technology. As a result Jordan has increased its trade with Western nations like the United States and joined the World Trade Organization.

Turkey, Malaysia, India, Indonesia, and China. In general, the goods that Jordan exports, or sells, are worth less than the goods that it imports, or buys. This has created an unfavorable balance of trade—in 2007 Jordan spent more than double on imports (about $12 billion) as it earned on imports (about $5.7 billion). Jordan has recently tried to improve its trade balance by exporting goods with higher value, like consumer goods and goods from the light-manufacturing sector. Pharmaceuticals and veterinary medicines are examples of this new direction.

In a sense, though, Jordan's most valuable export is skilled workers. Each year, Jordan receives a great sum of "invisible" income through remittances, money sent home to family members from Jordanians working abroad. This remittance income is a mainstay of economic growth in Jordan.

Large numbers of Jordanian workers go abroad for several reasons. In the first place, unemployment in Jordan is chronically high—recent estimates have put the figure between 25 and 30 percent—and professional jobs are particularly scarce. Yet Jordan has a relatively well-educated population. More than 30 percent of

Jordanians who leave their country to work abroad have university degrees. Most go to Saudi Arabia and other oil-producing countries.

Unlike many of its neighbors, Jordan has no oil reserves and relies on petroleum imports—principally from Saudi Arabia and Iraq—to fill its energy needs. However, natural gas was found in the northeastern part of Jordan in 1988, and there has been some prospecting for geothermal power resources.

Among the few natural resources that Jordan does have are phosphates, used in making fertilizers, and potash, which is made into industrial chemicals such as potassium chloride. The mining of both of these substances provides export income.

When Israel took the West Bank in 1967, Jordan lost some of its prime farmland. Today, less than 10 percent of Jordan's land can be used for farming, so agriculture is a small part of the overall economy. Given the country's limited water supply, this isn't likely to change. Jordan's main agricultural products are wheat, barley, maize, millet, lentils, beans, peas, sesame, tobacco, tomatoes, cucumbers, lemons, melons, cabbages, potatoes, onions, and bananas. Most vegetables are exported. In addition to these crops, Jordan produces some livestock. Chicken production meets the national demand for chicken meat and eggs, but 70 percent of the beef and lamb consumed in Jordan is imported. Jordan also needs to import staples such as grains.

Because of its limited possibilities for agriculture and scant natural resources, Jordan has developed its service industries. The country has made attempts to attract more foreign investment, and it has strengthened its own banking, insurance, and consulting businesses. Banking, in particular, is a strong service industry. Tourism is a growing industry in Jordan as well. In 1967, with the loss of the West Bank, Jordan lost most of its tourism revenue, which was, at the time, the country's greatest single source of income. But tourism has rebounded. Most visitors are from Arab countries, and the most popular destinations are the Nabatean ruins of Petra and the seacoast at Aqaba.

## GOVERNMENT

Jordan is considered more democratic than many other Arab nations. Its current constitution—put forth in 1952 and amended in 1974, 1976, and 1984—states that Jordan is a hereditary monarchy with a parliamentary form of government, defining the people as the source of its power. With a constitutional monarchy like that of Jordan, the monarch is the head of state. He is also the chief executive, signing or vetoing all laws passed by the legislature, and is the commander-in-chief of the military.

According to Jordan's constitution, the succession of the monarchy can change by decree. For many years, Hussein's brother Hassan was named his successor as Crown Prince. But before his death, Hussein dictated that his eldest son, Abdullah, would be his successor. King Abdullah is the fourth monarch in Jordan's history. His father, Hussein, did much to form a stable monarchy in a country where tribal loyalty, a sense of honor and revenge, and powerful religious beliefs were often at odds with the rule of law.

The constitution of Jordan divides the government into executive, legislative, and judicial powers and functions. The king has executive power and exercises authority with the help of his cabinet ministers, called the Council of Ministers. The National Assembly, the legislative body, is divided into the Senate, whose members are appointed by the king, and the House of Representatives, whose members are elected to four-year terms by the citizens of Jordan. Both the National Assembly and the king have legislative powers, which means that both can propose laws.

The Council of Ministers shares executive power with the monarch. However, the constitution requires that every new cabinet present a summary of programs and policies to the House of

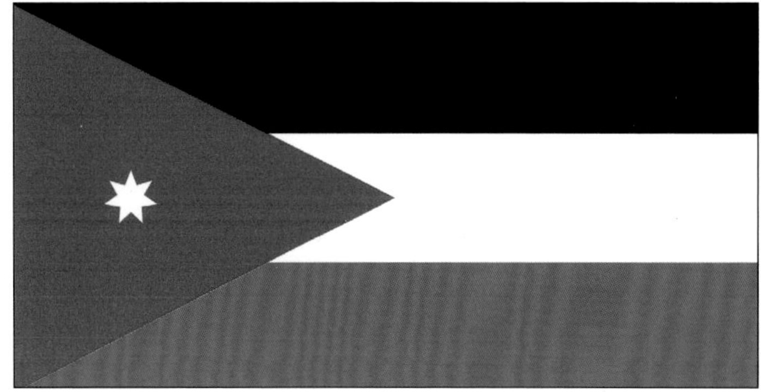

The flag of Jordan was adopted in 1928. It copies elements of a flag designed for the Arab Revolt by Sharif Hussein, father of Jordan's first king, Abdullah. The Jordanian flag adds a white star in the red field and changes the order of the horizontal colored stripes (in the Arab Revolt flag, the green stripe is above the white stripe). The flags of Iraq, Syria, and Kuwait also use a design modeled on the Revolt flag.

Representatives for a two-thirds vote of approval. Leading the Council of Ministers is the prime minister, who runs the government administration and appoints the cabinet to carry out tasks. Allegiance to the monarchy is an important factor in government service in Jordan, and historically more Transjordanians have served in positions of power than have Palestinians. Today, that pattern is beginning to change, with more Palestinian-Jordanians being given leading roles in government service.

All citizens over 18 have the right to vote. Palestinians can vote, but they must first give up their Palestinian nationality and choose Jordanian citizenship. For years, the constitutional right to vote meant very little in Jordan; between 1967 and 1989 no elections were held because the country was under martial law. During this time, political activity—including student activism, demonstrations, and political organizations—was severely restricted.

In 1991 a new election charter was ratified and implemented, permitting the legalization of political parties. Today there are more than 30 political parties in Jordan, including the National Constitutional Party, the Jordanian Democratic Popular Unity, and the Arab Land Party. There are a number of election laws that ensure minority groups are represented among the 110 representatives; nine seats are given to the Christians, Circassians, and Chechens and 10 to the Bedouins.

The constitution forbids discrimination on the basis of race, language, or religion, but the head of state and the prime minister must be Muslim.

On the local level, Jordan is divided into 12 districts, or governates, each overseen by a governor who is appointed by the minister of the interior. Within each district are cities and towns, which are governed by an elected mayor and council and are responsible for local concerns. Smaller villages are still governed by a ***mukhtar***, or headman. With the elimination of tribal law in 1976, the central government and its laws controlled even the most remote areas of Jordan.

The third branch of the Jordanian government is the judicial system. In Jordan, judicial powers are based on a combination of Islamic and European legal traditions. However, Jordan's law does not follow the *Sharia*, the Islamic law that some Muslim countries follow.

In Jordan, there are three kinds of courts: civil courts, which deal with most criminal and civil cases that don't fall under religious jurisdiction; religious courts, which deal with personal matters like inheritance and divorce; and special courts. Some special courts handle issues pertaining to military law, such as espionage. Also, there is a special court known as the Land Settlement Court, which deals with tribal law cases.

Judges are appointed by the king. A panel of three judges sits for all felony (serious criminal) trials; two judges sit for misdemeanor (minor criminal) and civil cases. In the Jordanian legal system there are no juries.

Jordanian law enforces the death penalty for murder, arson of an inhabited building, assassination (or attempted assassination) of the king, and other crimes that threaten state security. The highest court in Jordan is the Court of Cassation in Amman, which is somewhat similar to the U.S. Supreme Court. Its president serves as the chief justice of the country.

## RELIGION

The land that is now Jordan was one of the first areas to come under Islamic rule, in 633. Today more than 9 in 10 Jordanians is a Sunni Muslim. One of the two main branches of Islam, Sunni is practiced by about 90 percent of Muslims worldwide. In Jordan the other major branch of Islam, Shia, is practiced only by a very small number of people.

Both groups of Muslims share a belief in the importance of the Five Pillars of Islam, the fundamental elements of their faith. These obligations of prayer and faith—which must be performed with awareness, not out of habit—include *Shahada*, the statement that there is only one God and Muhammad was his last prophet; *Salat*, the prayer performed five times a day (at sunrise, midday, afternoon, sunset, and evening), during which the faithful bow and face the holy city of Mecca; *Zakat*, charitable donations to help the poor and to build and maintain mosques; *Sawm*, fasting from sunrise to sunset during the month of Ramadan; and *Hajj*, the pilgrimage to Mecca during the 12th month of the lunar calendar, a journey all Muslims are supposed to try to make at least once in their lifetime.

The spiritual, social, and ethical behavior of Sunni Muslims is guided by the Qur'an, which the faithful believe are the words of God as delivered to Muhammad; the Hadith, a collection of sayings and teachings attributed to Muhammad; and the *Sunna*, the example of Muhammad's personal behavior. For Muslims, moral conduct includes behavior that is generous, fair, honest, and respectful, especially in terms of family relations. Islam forbids adultery, gambling, usury, and the consuming of pork and alcohol. Friday is a day of prayer; on that day people do not work and usually go to the mosque to worship.

In traditional Islam there was no separation between religion and the state, or between religious law (*Sharia*) and secular law. In practice, however, modern Muslim countries—like their counterparts in the Western world—developed civil institutions that were at least partially independent of religion. But during the last decades of the 20th century, a movement to once again make Islam the basis of government, law, and society gained momentum in various Middle Eastern countries. Islamists—as those who favor this position are often called—came to power and established conservative Islamic governments in Iran in the late 1970s and Afghanistan in the 1990s, imposing *Sharia* and radically transforming their societies. Islamist movements exist in other Middle Eastern countries as well.

In Jordan civil institutions are firmly entrenched, though tensions exist between secular society and conservative Islam. Calls have been heard for a stricter observance of the *Sharia*. At various times Jordanian police have responded to Ramadan infractions, and observers have noted more women dressed in conservative Islamic attire. Since the 1980s, the influence of the Muslim Brotherhood, a conservative political and religious organization, has grown. For years the Muslim Brotherhood, which supported King Hussein, was permitted to operate in Jordan even when political parties were officially banned. But, more recently, its goals and those of the monarchy seem to have diverged, and some observers consider the Muslim Brotherhood a threat to Jordan's stability. The group has won popularity—particularly among Palestinians and the poor—by providing some social services and education, and by advocating jihad (holy war) against Israel.

Sunni Muslims participate in Friday prayers at a mosque in Amman. The split between Sunnis and Shiites originally stemmed from a controversy over who should succeed Muhammad as the leader of Islam after the Prophet's death in 632. Later doctrinal differences emerged. Shia Islam believes in a leader, called an *imam*, who is an infallible interpreter of the Qur'an and who has a divine right to lead. Sunnis believe that the *ulema*, a class of men of religious learning, have power to interpret the Qur'an.

### OTHER RELIGIONS

In addition to the Sunni Muslim majority, Jordan has various religious groups. Christians form the largest religious minority, accounting for about 6 percent of the population. Most share the Arabic language and culture; many are the descendants of the pre-Islamic Christian communities that dotted the landscape in ancient times. Armenians constitute the largest group of non-Arab Christians; most live in Irbid and Amman. The majority of Christians are part of the Eastern Orthodox churches; some are members of Greek Catholic churches or the Roman Catholic Church. Protestant churches are more recent and were established by European and American missionaries. The very small Shia Muslim minority is mostly descended from a 19th-century settlement of Chechen-Circassians, originally from the Caucasus Mountains in what is now part of the Russian Federation. Jordan also has a small community of Druze—members of a small, isolated sect of Islam—living near the Syrian border.

A falconer, near Ma'daba. Practically all of the people of Jordan are Arab Muslims, and Arabic culture predominates. Jordan has a population of more than 6 million; that number is growing at the fairly rapid rate of 2 percent a year (by contrast, the population growth rate in the United States is less than 1 percent).

# The People

Since its post–World War I beginnings, Jordan has seen tremendous changes in the size and makeup of its population. In 1921 fewer than 400,000 people inhabited the territory then called Transjordan. Most lived in villages in the highland region or were part of the nomadic Bedouin population. Today, the population of Jordan stands at more than 5 million, with the majority living in urban areas.

Before the 1940s the basic form of social organization in Jordan was the tribe. This held true especially for the nomadic Bedouins but also, to a certain extent, for villagers. Tribes consisted of related groups of families claiming descent from a founding ancestor. Arranged marriages helped maintain close family ties and tribal cohesiveness.

Sheikhs led the tribes of the desert areas. In villages—especially those of central and southern Jordan—a loose tribal structure also prevailed. The village leader was called a *mukhtar*, or headman.

Despite the huge shift in Jordan's population from rural to urban during the last half of the 20th century, tribal culture continues to influence modern Jordanian society. In 1985 King Hussein spoke of the importance of maintaining the traditions of tribal society: "Whatever harms tribes is considered harmful to us. Law will remain closely connected to norms, customs, and traditions . . . of the tribe. Our traditions should be made to preserve the fabric of society. Disintegration of tribes is very painful, negative and subversive." The major values of tribal culture include family loyalty, a strong sense of honor, and independence.

One of the factors that has most changed the face of Jordan's people is steady population growth, due to both a high birthrate and a steady influx of refugees. In Jordan, about one-third of the population is under the age of 15. Although the government encourages smaller families, that message goes against religion and custom. Continued Arab-Israeli conflict has produced a stream of Palestinian refugees. Another factor in the changing profile of Jordan's people has been the shift from rural to urban. As education became more widely available, the sons (and some daughters)

## The People of Jordan

**Population:** 6,198,677 (July 2008 est.)
**Ethnic groups:** Arab, 98%; Circassian, 1%; Armenian, 1%
**Age structure:**
0–14 years: 32.2%
15–64 years: 63.7%
65 years and over: 4.1%
**Population growth rate:** 2%
**Birth rate:** 20.13 births/1,000 population
**Death rate:** 2.72 deaths/1,000 population
**Infant mortality rate:** 15.57 deaths/1,000 live births
**Life expectancy at birth:**
total population: 78.71 years
males: 76.19 years
females: 81.39 years
**Total fertility rate:** 2.47 children born/woman
**Literacy:** 89.9% (2003 est.)

All figures are 2008 estimates unless otherwise indicated.
Source: CIA World Factbook, 2008

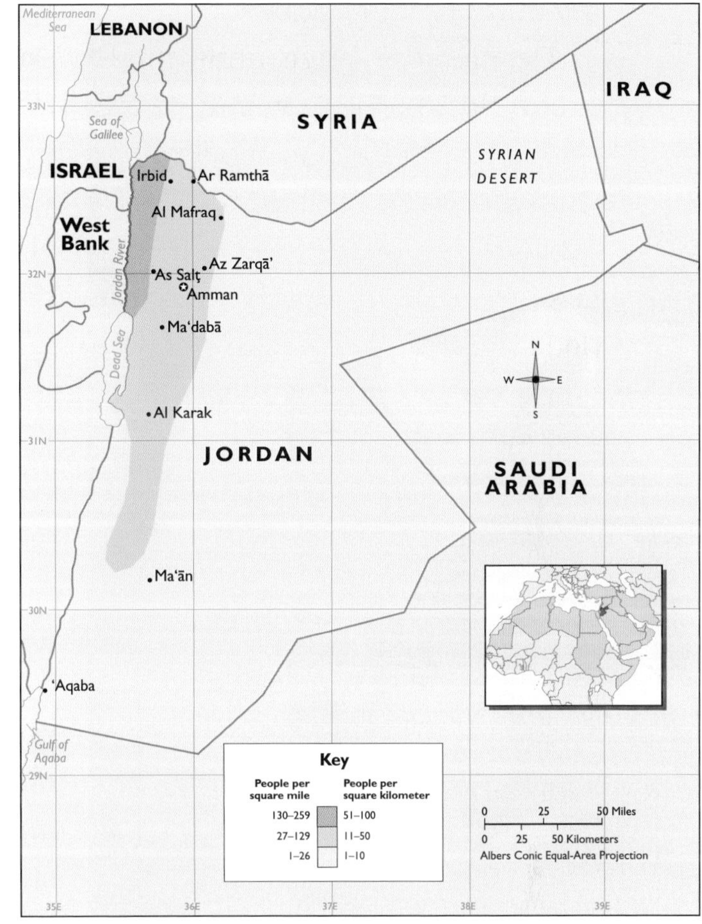


This map shows the distribution of people in Jordan. Most of the country's population lives in the Jordan River Valley. The nation's capital, Amman, is home to about 40 percent of Jordan's people.

of Bedouin nomads and village farmers went to Amman and other cities in search of work and opportunity.

## SIMILARITIES AND DIFFERENCES

Culturally, Jordan's people tend to be fairly similar to one another. The vast majority of Jordanians—even the nation's Christian minority—are Arabs and speak the Arabic language. The rhythms of Jordanian life are similar for most citizens. Businesses usually close in the heat of midday and stay open until nine or ten o'clock at night. The more than 9 in 10 Jordanians who are Sunni Muslims are further unified by the call to prayer five times a day. Another factor that unites Jordanians is the sense of being uprooted. Many

Bedouin children play with a camel in Petra. A camel calf stands behind them. Jordan's rural population has dropped steadily over the past few decades. In 1985, 36 percent of Jordanians lived in rural areas. By 1995 that figure had dropped to 28 percent; today about 25 percent of the population of Jordan lives in rural areas.

poorer people from rural areas moved to cities to find work, and Palestinian-Jordanians still feel connected to their lost homeland.

The biggest differences among Jordan's citizens are between urban and rural residents, and between the rich and the poor. Urban residents tend to be better educated and more Westernized than both Bedouins and other Arab country people. In the past, rural farmers and shepherds, whether they lived in villages in the Al Ghawr or roamed the desert near Ma'an, had little access to education and tended to be more traditional and poorer. However, by the late 1980s, the educational gap had narrowed, and the size of the rural population continued to drop. These social divisions, as well as distinctions between Palestinian or Jordanian ancestry and tribal affiliation, tend to cut across class divisions of rich and poor.

In Jordan, as in the rest of the world, a large gap exists between rich and poor. Jordan's richest 10 percent consume about 35 percent of the nation's wealth; its poorest 10 percent, less than 2.5 percent. An estimated 3 in 10 Jordanians live below the poverty line. Wealthy Jordanians travel extensively, live in luxurious residences, have domestic help, and resemble their American or European counterparts as much as their fellow Jordanians. The people at the top of the economic pyramid, representing the smallest group of the Jordanian population, are large landowners, industrialists, and leading financial figures. On the second level are professionals, such as doctors and lawyers, army officers, and government officials. Next in economic rank are the white-collar workers and schoolteachers. Below them are the shopkeepers and artisans. At the bottom of the economic pyramid are the unemployed, whose numbers have grown in recent years. Education for professional work is the key factor in class mobility.

### PALESTINIAN-JORDANIANS

In general, Jordan's city-dwellers tend to be of Palestinian ancestry, and most live in the Amman region. Overall, some sources estimate, about 60 percent of Jordan's population is of Palestinian origin.

Violence has contributed greatly to Palestinian immigration to Jordan. In the 1920s, conflict with Zionist settlers motivated some Palestinians to move eastward across the Jordan River. During the Arab-Israeli war of 1948, many Palestinians whose villages were destroyed or who were driven forcibly from their land went to Jordan. And the 1967 Six-Day War produced a staggering quarter-million West Bank refugees.

Many Palestinian immigrants to Jordan, particularly those who arrived after the 1948 and 1967 wars, were well-educated urbanites whose attitudes and business skills did much to modernize the culture and economy of Jordan. Arriving with money and skills, they tended to assimilate easily into the Jordanian population. By contrast, Palestinians from rural areas, possessing little education and few business skills, had a much more difficult time fitting into Jordanian culture. Many of these people spent years living in refugee camps.

The Palestinian-Jordanian sense of national identity has been the subject of much debate. Before the 1960s, there really was no strong sense of a Palestinian identity because the political talk of the times focused on Arab unity. The creation of the PLO changed that, and today Palestinian-Jordanians living in the East Bank may define themselves as Jordanian or as Palestinian. The most militant Palestinians tend to be the poorest and the most recent arrivals to Jordan, living in refugee camps. Overall about one-quarter of Palestinian-Jordanians live in refugee camps.

### Bedouins

Although they make up less than 3 percent of the total population of Jordan, the Bedouin minority is very important to Jordanian society. Many Jordanians see the roots of their national identity in the surviving remnants of Bedouin tribal culture.

Before Jordan became a country—indeed, from ancient times—the Bedouins were the only residents of the desert and oases outside the East Bank region. National boundaries meant little to them in their migrations. They camped for a few months at a time in one spot, letting their herds of goats, sheep, or cattle graze. When the fodder ran out, they moved on. Traditional Bedouins lived in goat-hair tents, which often had two rooms, one for women and the other for men. Camels provided their main means of transport.

Today most nomadic tribes are found in the desert areas east of a line running from Al Mafraq to Ma‘an. Some semi-nomadic groups are found near the Al Ghawr region and Irbid. Bedouins are among

Jordan's poorest groups; many Bedouin men hold menial jobs in desert towns, and many women sell rugs to tourists. Other Bedouin men have translated their nomadic ways to modern life—many have become truck drivers.

**The largest Bedouin tribes are the Bani Sukhurs, Hawayatats, and Sirhans. The Bedouins of Ma'an were romanticized in the 1926 book *The Seven Pillars of Wisdom*, by the British officer T. E. Lawrence. Along with King Abdullah, Lawrence led the Bedouins to battle against the Ottoman Turks during World War I.**

Most Bedouins have become more sedentary as government policies have encouraged settlement. In Ma'an tribal members now live in cement-block houses, although many people still prefer to sleep outdoors in tents. In exchange for giving up their traditional way of life, the Bedouins have gotten access to schools, water, and health care. Although their lives are more settled now, many retain old desert values and practices, including the segregation of gender, arranged marriages, loyalty to clan, a strict code of honor, and the importance of hospitality.

### OTHER MINORITIES

Jordan's Arab Christians have lived alongside their Muslim neighbors without conflict for centuries. Many can trace their roots back to the Roman era. Although they make up only about 6 percent of the population, Christians tend to be disproportionately prosperous because they have had access to Western-style education for generations.

Circassians and Chechens, who are Muslim but not Arab, make up Jordan's other significant minority. The ancestors of these people came from the region in southern Russia now known as

Chechnya. In the mid-19th century the Ottomans, trying to balance Bedouin influence and gain control in the region, resettled members of these two tribes in the Jordan region. The Circassians and Chechens settled in Amman and built the neighboring city of Az Zarqa. Though economically successful, they remain somewhat separate culturally from the Arab majority.

### The Family

At the center of Jordanian culture is the family, which for most Jordanians forms the basis for their social life and their sense of identity. In Jordan "family" often refers to an extended family, and a household can include a married couple, unmarried children, and other relatives. Extended families provide tremendous economic and emotional support, and family traditions remain strong. But recent changes in attitude have begun to challenge the Jordanian family's traditional role. These changes include greater individualism among educated young people, a desire among women for more freedom, and an increased emphasis on romantic love in marriage.

Nevertheless, in many parts of Jordan marriage is still perceived as a family choice, not a personal decision. Arranged marriages continue to be part of Bedouin life, and even urban people will consult with their families before marrying. Islam permits men to have as many as four wives, and the custom of taking multiple wives existed among Arabs before the time of Muhammad. Women, however, may have only one husband at a time. For Muslims, it is harder for a woman to divorce than for a man.

### The Place of Women

As in other Muslim countries, gender separation is part of Jordanian culture. Although men and women now interact in public at school, in the workplace, on public transportation, and at some social events, the social lives of men and women tend to be

Women in traditional garb read in a library in Amman. Although women in Jordan have more freedom than women in some other Arab countries, many choose the traditional female role in Islamic lands—staying at home to raise a family, rather than working, for example.

separate. Because of household responsibilities, women are more restricted to the home. Among better-off members of society, houses have separate areas for men and women. These houses have a reception area for men and their guests, as well as separate quarters for women where the only males permitted are relatives and servants. In the past, rules about gender separation tended to be stricter among the urban middle class and looser among the Bedouin, a reflection of the pressures of nomadic life. Traditionally, segregation was part of the concept of honor and reputation: keeping women apart from men diminished chances for a family's loss of honor.

The value of female modesty and privacy remains high in Muslim culture. A visitor to Amman would see many women dressed in Western-style clothes, but some would be wearing scarves and full-length long-sleeved dresses. Traditional Islamic law requires women not to expose anything more than their face, hands, and ankles. In the 1980s, with the revival of fundamentalist Islam throughout the Middle East, many Jordanian women—even students and workingwomen—began wearing Islamic dress.

Women's roles in Jordan have changed slowly. Although many women now go to college, few are actually in the workforce. Most workingwomen are in traditionally female professions, such as teaching or nursing. In 1993, however, Tousan Faisal achieved a milestone, becoming the first Jordanian woman elected to the

Jordanian brides and grooms prepare for a mass wedding ceremony at a school in Amman, July 20, 2001. The wedding ceremony for 72 couples was organized by an Islamic charity, which invited some 5,000 people to attend the rare event.

A Jordanian woman prepares a meal, which will be cooked in a fireplace made from stones, Petra.

House of Representatives.

Women have made further strides in the political arena—women must fill eight seats in the House of Representatives. But it is still common to see most women married by the age of 20. And single women typically live with their extended families and are discouraged from living alone.

## Food

Because families are at the center of Jordanian social life, eating meals together is very important. Jordan has few grocery stores; most women must shop every day for food, going to small specialty shops such as bakeries or butcher shops. Lunch is the biggest meal of the day and the preferred time for visiting with friends and family. Men often go to restaurants and coffeehouses with friends in the afternoon and evening.

Typical foods served in a Jordanian home include various combinations of lamb, yogurt, chicken, bulgur, parsley, eggplant, garlic, tomatoes, and rice. Flat bread—made from wheat flour, water, and salt but no yeast—is used to scoop up food. Olives are served at almost every meal. Dates are an important sweetener. Traditional sweets are made from nuts, coconut, and spun sugar. A typical dish of Bedouin origin is *mansif*, which is made from yogurt, lamb, and rice, simmered together for a long time. Fast foods, sold at shops

Jordanian schoolchildren hold pictures of King Abdullah and the late King Hussein at a May 2000 parade in Amman to celebrate the 54th anniversary of independence from Great Britain. Jordan has one of the best-educated populations in the Arab world; almost 90 percent of Jordanians over the age of 15 can read and write.

and by street vendors, include *sharwarma* (lamb or chicken, plus condiments rolled in a flat bread), kebabs (made from spiced, minced lamb), and falafel (chick pea croquettes rolled in flat bread).

## Education

Although Transjordan had a largely illiterate population in 1922, Jordan today has one of the highest literacy rates in the Middle East. Its system of education improved greatly during the reign of King Hussein. The Ministry of Education sets the national curriculum, and the law requires all children to attend school through the 10th grade.

The primary curriculum includes reading and writing in Arabic, religion, arithmetic, civics and history, geography, science, music, physical education, drawing for boys, and embroidery for girls. English is added to the curriculum in the fifth grade.

Jordan has 21 universities. In recent years, the government has made significant strides in creating new universities, which has helped expand higher education. The government continues to develop new and improve existing education programs.

### LITERATURE AND THE ARTS

The art of writing has been practiced in the Middle East since ancient times; in fact, the alphabet was a Middle Eastern invention. Not surprisingly, literature has long been considered an important art form in Arabic culture. Classical Arabic literature used poetic forms, coming from the Bedouin oral tradition. One form of classical poetry was the *quasidah.* These poems followed a specific formula—they were usually about a journey and lost love. Jordanians continue to enjoy classical literature, but modern poets and novelists are also widely read. Much modern literature in Jordan has been inspired by the conflict over Palestine and treats the suffering of the displaced Palestinian people.

Traditional and contemporary musical forms also continue to be popular in Jordan. Traditional music, played on lute-like stringed instruments such as the *oud* and the *kemancha,* was an important part of many occasions, including the harvest, marriage, and war. Rural people continue to play this music during festivals, but it is also preserved by cultural societies in urban areas. Modern Arabic music uses an orchestra. Jordanian teenagers, like their counterparts in Western countries, listen to pop and rock.

Traditional handicrafts are still part of Jordanian culture. Fine metalwork can be found in the gold and silver jewelry that has been made and worn by Bedouins for centuries. Woodworkers continue to create ornamental carvings, such as the screen mosaics that are a recognizable part of Islamic architecture. Jordanian weavers still produce beautiful wool rugs. Traditionally, Bedouins used rugs instead of furniture, but most rugs produced today are for export.

GLASS BOAT

Jordanians relax on the beach at Aqaba, located on the Red Sea near the Hejaz Mountains and the southern border with Saudi Arabia. The historic city, Jordan's fifth largest, is the country's only seaport.

# Communities

The eastern part of Jordan is located within an area known as the Fertile Crescent, a semicircular swath of land stretching from the southeastern Mediterranean coast around the Syrian Desert through Iraq all the way to the Persian Gulf. In ancient times this area gave birth to agriculture, which over thousands of years transformed hunter-gatherer societies into urban civilizations.

Jordan itself contains none of the ancient cities where urban life began and thrived continuously for thousands of years, however. Cairo, Baghdad, Jerusalem, and Damascus—all of these cities in neighboring lands have their roots in the prehistoric cultures that planted the seeds of urban life. While these cities grew, coming under the influence of various empires that rose and fell, the region that is now Jordan remained largely rural, inhabited by villagers and nomads. Its few towns were merely stopping points on caravan routes.

When these routes shifted, the towns faded.

Today most of Jordan's population lives in urban areas concentrated in the highland region, and the nation's culture is dominated by the presence of several thriving modern cities. Jordan has adapted to the modern world with fewer difficulties than many other nations of the Middle East. Overall, Jordanians are better educated and more cosmopolitan than their Arab neighbors. However, amid the country's increasing urbanization, some traditional values have been lost. Such values include the obligation of the rich to care for the poor. In Jordan's cities—as in cities all over the world—wealthy residents who enjoy all the amenities of a Western lifestyle go about their business while the urban poor struggle to find employment, decent housing, and health care.

### Amman

Jordan's capital as well as its largest city, Amman is a mixture of many different elements. On the site of an ancient village founded beside a riverbed, the modern city—which lacks a traditional center—has spread out to the seven surrounding hills, connected by wide boulevards, overpasses, and tile-lined tunnels. Today, Amman boasts more than two million residents, nearly half of Jordan's total population.

Modern Amman sits on the site of Rabboth Ammon, the capital of a tribe mentioned in the Bible, the Ammonites. When the ancient caravan routes shifted away from Rabboth Ammon, however, the thriving trade center slowly disappeared until all that remained was a village. One thousand years later, this village had grown into the Greco-Roman city of Philadelphia. During the Roman era, it became a wealthy market town, but its importance faded when the Roman Empire became weak.

Early in the Islamic era, the city flourished anew as a trade center, but once again shifting caravan routes brought about another

Amman, often called the White City, is capital of the Hashemite Kingdom of Jordan. When King Abdullah I moved his government there in the early 1920s, Amman was a small town. Over the years it expanded to cover the surrounding hills, and today Amman boasts a population of more than two million.

gradual decline, until the settlement was abandoned in the 15th century to famine and plague. In the 19th century the Ottomans settled several thousand Chechen and Circassian Muslims fleeing persecution by the Russian czar in Amman. The new arrivals established themselves near the old Roman amphitheater, setting up businesses and building roads. The town remained Circassian until the building of the railroad to Mecca, which brought with it several thousand Arabs. When Abdullah I decided to make it his capital, the town experienced some growth. But by 1943, Amman still had only 30,000 inhabitants.

After 1948 the population of Amman grew rapidly in response to the flood of refugees from Palestine. Because of the influx of

Palestinians, who were more Westernized and better educated than their Jordanian neighbors, Amman became a thoroughly modern city. More Palestinian refugees came during the 1967 and 1973 Arab-Israeli wars. During the Gulf War in 1991, Palestinians working in Iraq and Kuwait flocked to Amman.

As the population of Jordan's capital grew, Amman's importance as the cultural and political center of the nation increased. During the reign of King Hussein, much care was given to urban planning. Many trees were planted, restrictions were placed on the height of buildings so that the city would be filled with sunlight, and buildings were required to be white or light sandstone, making the city look clean and bright. Other features of urban planning that make Amman an attractive city are the absence of superhighways and the availability of good water and sewage treatment.

Not surprisingly, given that the government is Jordan's largest employer, many residents of Amman, the nation's capital, hold government jobs. Other major industries include banking and finance and insurance. Jordan's largest university is in Amman as well, making it a center for higher education.

Amman is a very attractive modern city, boasting some beautiful Arabic-Mediterranean architecture and contemporary high-rise buildings. But the old sections of the city are also charming and attract tourists. Old Amman has a 6,000-seat amphitheater built by the Romans, and a labyrinth of tiny shops along streets laid out by Arabs who arrived at the beginning of the 20th century.

### Az Zarqa

With a population of about 480,000, Az Zarqa is the second-largest city in Jordan. Originally a suburb of Amman, it is located just a few miles northeast of the capital city. Although the remnants of Neolithic and Bronze Age communities have been found nearby, Az Zarqa's existence as a city is quite recent. Like Amman,

Az Zarqa was originally a village that grew into a town after the arrival of Circassian migrants in the 19th century.

While Amman's economy is driven by the service industries of government and finance, Az Zarqa is one of Jordan's most important industrial centers. It has the country's only oil refinery, as well as the power plant that supplies much of northern Jordan's electricity. In 1991 Az Zarqa became home to the Hashemite University, part of the expansion of Jordan's national system of higher education.

### IRBID

Irbid is the third-largest city in Jordan, with a population of more than 300,000. The northernmost urban center in the country, it is located just a few miles from the borders with Syria and Lebanon. This has given the city strategic importance, and Jordan has military bases there.

Culturally, Irbid's importance to Jordan was enhanced by its becoming the site of Yarmuk University. That institution of higher education was established in 1976.

The population of Irbid is more mixed than that of other cities in Jordan. Besides residents of Palestinian and Transjordanian descent, the families of many people originally came from Syrian towns, such as Damascus, before the 20th century. In addition, unlike most Jordanian towns, Irbid was never organized tribally, with clans headed by sheikhs.

Archaeological evidence shows that Irbid has been inhabited since the Bronze Age, around 4000 B.C. Throughout its history Irbid has been part of the agricultural center of the country, located within the triangle formed by the Jordan, Zarqa, and Yarmuk Rivers. Historically, Irbid was the main market town of this grain-producing region, oriented toward trade with Syrian merchants. However, its growth as a city is relatively recent. Some newer industries, such as the pharmaceutical industry, are based in Irbid.

### RUSSEIFA

One of the highland communities near Amman that emerged as a city in the late 20th century, Russeifa today has a population of around 270,000, making it Jordan's fourth-largest city. Originally a small agricultural community, Russeifa grew primarily because of the development of the phosphate mining and processing industry. This industry has been very important to Jordan's economy; phosphates, which are used in fertilizers, are one of the nation's only natural resources and provide a significant part of its export income.

### AQABA

Once the great Islamic port of Ayla, today Aqaba is a small but thriving city on the Red Sea. It holds the distinction of being Jordan's only port. With a population of 140,000, it is also the country's fifth-largest city. Located along Jordan's very short stretch of coastline, Aqaba is only a few miles from both the Israeli and Saudi borders.

Historically, Aqaba rose and fell with the waves of conquerors that continually swept through the region. The Crusaders wrested the port of Ayla from its Islamic keepers, and in 1099, they built a fortress on Pharaoh Island, just off the coast of the city. During the Ottoman period, Aqaba was neglected and largely forgotten by the outside world. Its importance as a trade center faded, and it became a small fishing town. Aqaba regained strategic importance during the Arab Revolt, and in 1917, British troops occupied the city, using it as a base from which to overthrow the Ottomans in this region.

Today, Aqaba is the site of much economic activity. It is the center of the Jordanian shipping industry, and it has good road and rail connections to Amman. While there is a small fishing industry based in Aqaba, its second most important industry, after shipping, is tourism. With 360 days of sunshine a year, Aqaba's beaches are a major attraction for wealthy tourists, mostly from the Middle East.

### OTHER COMMUNITIES

Other urban centers in the highland region are Ma'daba, with a population of about 87,000; As Salt, with a population of about 80,000; and Ar Ramtha, with a population of about 88,000. Their growth from towns to small cities occurred in the late 20th century, as industry from Amman and Az Zarqa overflowed throughout the highland region.

With a population of less than 30,000, Ma'an—located at the southern end of the high plateau in western Jordan—is less a city than a town. But it has a historical importance that goes beyond its size. King Abdullah I, the founder of Jordan, went first to Ma'an to establish a connection with the tribal population who lived there. These people have been the most loyal supporters of the Hashemite monarchy throughout Jordan's relatively brief history. Today, most of Ma'an's citizens are settled and semi-settled Bedouins. The town has little industry and few high-rise buildings, but it is a jumping-off point for tourists interested in visiting the nearby ruins of Petra.

Outside of its urban centers, Jordan continues to have a significant population of Palestinians living in refugee camps. Given the current state of unrest in Palestinian communities, getting an accurate figure for this population is difficult. However, in the 1990s more than 200,000 Palestinians lived in refugee camps. The largest, Bequ'a, has more than 70,000 residents and is located near Amman. Refugee camps are often organized around the former village populations that live there. Today, a *mukhtar*, the traditional village leader, usually looks after the interests of his village's people in refugee camps, just as he did when they lived in their original village in Palestine. While many refugees eventually integrate into the general population of Jordan and accept Jordanian citizenship, others stay in the camps, hoping one day to return to their original homeland.

## FESTIVALS

In Jordan, most festivals are celebrations connected to births, weddings, and religious traditions. Special music and dancing also mark plowing, planting, and harvesting in rural areas. In the countryside, there are festivals for Muslim saints at the tomb or traditional residence of the saint. These festivals resemble country fairs and may include traditional dancing. Folk dances that Jordanians participate in during festival time include the *debkah*, in which dancers move in flamenco-like steps, accompanied by drums and clapping hands.

Because family life is so important in Arab culture, weddings are huge celebrations. For many people, their wedding is the most significant event in their lives, involving their entire community. Women from tribal backgrounds painstakingly prepare special embroidered clothing for their day as a bride. Before the wedding ceremony, men and women celebrate separately. After the ceremony, feasting, socializing, and dancing can last for several days. Again, women and men often celebrate separately.

Throughout the Middle East, Muslim religious festivals are the most important celebrations throughout the year. During Ramadan, fasting all day ends with a feast after sunset called an *iftar*. Special foods, made only during Ramadan, are eaten. Some of these special foods include traditional sweets made from dates. After Ramadan ends, there is a three-day celebration called Eid al-Fitr, in which people wear new clothes for feasting and visiting friends and family. Another important festival, Eid al-Adha, is observed after the hajj, the pilgrimage to Mecca. It commemorates the willingness of Ibrahim (Abraham) to sacrifice his son and today includes a feast.

A Palestinian family in the Bequ'a refugee camp in Jordan, 1977. Today an estimated 1.4 million Palestinians live in refugee camps in Jordan. Early waves of Palestinian refugees arrived in Jordan in 1947–1948, and again in 1967–1968.

Dates for these festivals are set by the Islamic calendar and change each year with respect to the Gregorian, or Western, calendar. That is because the Islamic calendar is based on lunar cycles—each month begins when the crescent moon first becomes visible to a human observer after a new moon. Because the Islamic year is slightly longer than 354 days, Muslim holidays shift back with respect to the Gregorian calendar about 11 days each year. For example, the Islamic New Year fell on March 15 in 2002 (the year 1423 in the Islamic calendar, which begins A.D. 622), but in 2007 (1428 in the Islamic calendar) it will fall around January 21.

Islamic celebrations are very important in Jordan, as they bring together most of the population, who share a common identity as Muslims. Differences between Jordanians and Palestinians, between different tribes, between the rich and the poor, become insignificant in the atmosphere of celebration. The country is united by these common experiences of faith and good will.

Israeli police arrest Palestinian demonstrators in the West Bank, 1988. The *intifada* forced Jordan to renounce its claim on the West Bank territory. Over the years the Hashemite rulers have carefully weighed the effects of their foreign policies on other Arab nations, Israel, and the West.

# Foreign Relations

Jordan, a small, resource-poor country in a turbulent region, has pursued a foreign policy balancing the demands of three separate, sometimes conflicting, areas of concentration: Palestine and Israel, the Middle East, and the nations of the West. Much of Jordan's foreign policy was developed in response to the Arab-Israeli conflict, and Jordan has sought Arab unity as a way to make peace with Israel. At the same time, Jordan's dependence on foreign aid has shaped much of its foreign policy with both wealthier Arab nations and the West. Finally, its position as a moderate pro-Western government on the front lines of the Arab-Israeli struggle has made national security a constant concern.

## Uneasy Relations with the PLO

Jordan's most complex relationship is with Palestine, the PLO, and the Palestinian people. For many years, the boundary between the Palestinians and the Jordanians was as unresolved as the border between the West Bank and Jordan. Like Jordan's founder, Abdullah, King Hussein believed that Jordanians and Palestinians were the same people, united by the eastern Arab ideals of nationalism that his great-grandfather stood for. This made Jordan both an advocate and an enemy of the Palestinian cause since the 1960s. Until 1988, when Jordan renounced its claim on the West Bank, the PLO and Jordan were in conflict over who best represented the interests of the Palestinian people.

During the PLO's early years, King Hussein tolerated the organization's presence on Jordanian territory—even though Palestinian incursions into Israel frequently brought Israeli retaliation upon Jordan. After Yasir Arafat took control of the PLO, however, the threat to the king's rule became more acute. Hussein—along with other Arab states—had helped establish bases for and equip the fedayeen in their struggle with Israel. But Arafat was not content simply to operate from his bases. The PLO armed and organized Palestinians living in refugee camps in Jordan. And, most alarming from King Hussein's point of view, Arafat established a virtual state-within-a-state around the Jordanian capital of Amman. He and his fedayeen flouted Jordanian authority and, after a series of clashes with government troops, began advocating the king's overthrow. In September 1970, on the heels of a spate of airplane hijackings carried out by Palestinian terrorists, King Hussein took action. He ordered his army to crack down on the PLO. In the ensuing civil war, the Jordanian army decisively defeated Arafat's fedayeen. Hussein and Arafat signed a peace agreement, but much tension remained, and the king lost support in the Arab world.

In 1974, at a conference of Arab states, the PLO was made the official representative of the Palestinian people. Only Jordan objected, arguing that the PLO was incapable of taking Palestine from

King Abdullah II greets Palestinian president Mahmoud Abbas in Amman on December 3, 2007. The two have met on several occasions to help bring peace and stability to the region. Abbas replaced former PLO leader Yasir Arafat as the leader of the Palestinians.

Israel by military means or of negotiating a peace settlement. In spite of this obvious lack of faith, King Hussein tried to create a joint Palestinian-Jordanian position from which to negotiate with Israel, and he attempted to get the PLO to accept UN Resolution 242. However, Arafat, pressured perhaps by radical elements within the PLO, refused. The relationship between Jordan and the PLO deteriorated during the 1980s, and in 1986 Hussein cut off all dealings with Arafat.

The turning point came in 1988 during the Palestinian uprising in the West Bank. Hussein gave up legal or administrative claims to the land and called for the PLO to assume responsibility for the area. By the end of the year, the PLO had announced the independence of Palestine and accepted UN Resolution 242.

Arafat died on November 11, 2004, and his successor, Mahmoud Abbas, was eventually elected as the new leader of the Palestine Authority. Over the past few years, Abbas and Abdullah have met on a number of occasions to discuss ways to stabilize the relationship between the two countries and to attempt to keep things peaceful in the Middle East.

### JORDANIAN-ISRAELI RELATIONS

Like its relationship with Palestinians and the PLO, Jordan's relationship with Israel has been very complex, particularly since 1967. While technically at war from 1948 until 1994, Jordan and Israel maintained over many years a secret dialogue for pragmatic purposes. In so doing they managed to avoid further warfare.

In dealing with the Israelis, King Hussein walked an extremely fine line. Had the dialogue become known, his powerful Arab neighbors—not to mention hundreds of thousands of Palestinians living within his borders—would have been angered. So the king had to be careful to publicly support the Palestinian cause. At the same time, Hussein needed the cooperation of Israel to pursue important goals, such as regaining lost land—and even keeping control of his kingdom. And Jordan could exert little direct pressure, either military or economic, on its powerful neighbor.

At one time, Israel had pursued policies that gravely threatened Hussein's rule. During the 1970s Prime Minister Menachem Begin had advocated Israeli annexation of the West Bank—with the idea that the Palestinians who lived there should immigrate to Jordan and overthrow the Hashemite monarchy. Among the most enthusiastic promoters of this idea was Ariel Sharon, who held various cabinet posts under the conservative Likud Party government.

In the 1980s, however, the plan lost support. Major Israeli political leaders, including Sharon, now recognized the need for Jordan as a buffer state. Perhaps because of the king's willingness to maintain the secret dialogue that had begun before Israel became a state, they saw the Hashemite monarchy as less hostile to Israel, and more stable, than a possible government run by the PLO.

For his part, Hussein had strong reasons for wanting to establish a relationship with Israel, in spite of the lack of resolution in the overall Arab-Israeli conflict. Jordan shares the longest border with Israel of any Arab state. This border has made Jordan vulnerable to attacks by the most powerful military in the Middle East. In 1967 Israel demonstrated its superior military might, and it continued to show its strength in attacks on Palestinian targets in Tunisia, Lebanon, and Syria in the following years. Jordan, for its own security, needed a working relationship with Israel. In addition, the two nations had areas of joint interest, including sharing irrigation technologies, water resources, and energy projects in the Dead Sea. Another reason for cooperation was the close ties between Palestinians living in Jordan and the Israeli-occupied West Bank. The "open bridges" policy between Israel and Jordan allowed people and goods to move back and forth with relative freedom. Access to Jordan allowed Palestinians to stay connected to relatives who were refugees throughout the Arab world.

Before 1988 neither Israel nor Jordan wanted to see the establishment of a Palestinian state in the West Bank. Jordan hoped to regain the area. Many Israelis, especially from conservative and religious parties, advocated the increased building of Jewish settlements in the West Bank—as a prelude, Arab critics charged, to annexation. While Israeli actions were roundly condemned by leaders of the Arab world, Hussein avoided drawing criticism by keeping his goals obscure. He was aware that he would alienate his Arab neighbors by presuming to speak for the Palestinian people in the peace process. However, from 1984 to 1986, King Hussein worked with Israeli prime minister Shimon Peres to increase the Jordanian presence in the West Bank in order to offset the power of the PLO there. They began to secretly work out an arrangement by which Jordan and Israel would jointly administer the West Bank.

The Palestinian *intifada* that began in December 1987 dramatically changed King Hussein's thinking. In 1988 he decided to relinquish

Israeli prime minister Yitzhak Rabin and Jordanian prime minister Abdul Salam Majali sign a peace treaty in the fall of 1994; U.S. president Bill Clinton, seated between the two leaders, witnesses the historic document. Jordan became the second Arab nation to sign a treaty with Israel, following Egypt (1979).

his goal of Jordanian sovereignty in the West Bank. This decision greatly simplified Jordan's relationship with Israel. Freed from the need to balance the concerns of the Palestinian people with Jordan's national interests, he could pursue open negotiations with Israel. In the months that followed, negotiations over water rights, refugees, and other concerns took place, eventually paving the way for the peace agreement Jordan and Israel signed in 1994.

Since the signing of the peace agreement, Jordan has maintained a generally cordial relationship with Israel. After Hussein's death in 1999, King Abdullah continued his father's policies. Even after the second Palestinian *intifada*, which began in September 2000, Abdullah pressed for a working relationship with Israel among Arab states. Continued conflict between the Israelis and Palestinians has complicated that goal, however. Abdullah has tended to side with other Arab states that condemn Israel's anti-terrorist actions as aggression against a suffering nation.

## Jordanian Leadership in the Arab World

Largely because of the question of Palestine, Jordan's foreign relations with its Arab neighbors were often strained before 1988. Today, Jordan maintains friendly relations with most Arab states; its closest ties are with Egypt, Iraq, Kuwait, and Saudi Arabia. Following the foreign policy established by his father, King Abdullah often meets with leaders in these countries to discuss regional strategies.

By the 1980s King Hussein's skills as a diplomat and his thoughtful foreign policy began to give Jordan an important voice in the Arab world. In 1984 Jordan became the first Arab country to reestablish diplomatic relations with Egypt, which allowed the two nations to become extremely close allies. In 1987 Hussein hosted the Arab League summit in Amman.

By the end of the 1980s, Jordan had become a leader in foreign policy in the region. In 1989 Egypt and Jordan joined with Iraq and the Yemen Arab Republic to form the new Arab Cooperation Council. During the Gulf War of 1991, King Hussein chose not to ally Jordan with the U.S.-led coalition seeking to oust Iraq from Kuwait, even though that meant a devastating loss in foreign aid. The king favored negotiations between Kuwait and Iraq, a nation with which Jordan maintained close economic ties.

## Conflicts with Syria

Historically, Jordan's most strained relations in the Arab world have been with Syria. The problems have deep roots. While Jordan became a parliamentary monarchy and enjoyed support from

Western nations, Syria developed as a socialist state, with a history of hostility toward the West. Adding to the tension is the fact that most of Jordan's population and agricultural land are concentrated in the northwest corner of the country, where they are vulnerable to potential Syrian aggression.

In September 1970, Syrian troops did cross into Jordan. They sought to aid Palestinian guerrillas fighting the Jordanian army, but were soon forced to withdraw. In 1979 Syria accused Jordan of stirring up religious violence within its borders. By the following year the relationship between the two countries had broken down completely, and Saudi Arabia attempted to mediate. For the next five years tensions remained high, with Jordan accusing Syria of backing Palestinian assassination plots. Saudi Arabia helped to restore diplomatic relations between the feuding Arab nations in 1986, but new difficulties emerged in the 1990s. Syria was very critical of Jordan's peace agreement with Israel; even today, Syrians interpret Jordan's peace with the Jewish state as evidence that Jordan is a pawn of the United States.

The only other country that Jordan has had difficult relations with in recent times is Iran. Jordan cut off diplomatic relations in 1981 in support of Iraq during the Iran-Iraq war.

Jordan has had good relations with most other Middle Eastern countries, especially the Persian Gulf states. Jordan receives most of its foreign aid from these countries—in particular, Saudi Arabia. Also, Jordan sends many people to the Gulf as skilled workers in the oil industry. The remittances from these workers are an important part of the Jordanian economy.

### U.S.-Jordanian Ties

Jordan has historically enjoyed friendly relations with most European countries and with the United States. Jordan's close ties with the United States date to 1957, when America replaced Britain

King Abdullah meets with President George W. Bush at the White House in August 2002. The two leaders spoke about tensions in the Middle East. Although Jordan has a strong relationship with the United States, the country has followed its own foreign policy path.

as the main source of Jordan's Western foreign aid. At that time, U.S. policy was to ensure Jordan's continued independence and stability. American aid helped in equipping and maintaining Jordan's military. During the civil war of 1970, Washington strongly supported King Hussein, which caused strong anti-American sentiment among Palestinians in Jordan and elsewhere. In 1974 U.S. "shuttle diplomacy"—directed at resolving issues from the 1973 Yom Kippur War—included Egypt and Syria, but not Jordan. Over the next 10 years, the close ties between the United States and Israel pushed Jordan to develop a foreign policy separate from U.S. interests.

The Gulf War of 1991 created another rift between Jordan and the United States. At the war's end, however, Jordan worked successfully to reestablish a cordial relationship with its American ally. However, the relationship was strained when the United States invaded Iraq in 2003. Jordan had an agreement with the regime of Saddam Hussein to receive oil grants, and when he was removed from power, Jordan was cut off. The government had to seek alternative solutions for resources—but it still remained a loyal ally to the United States. In fact, in 2008 King Abdullah became the first Arab leader to visit Iraq following the invasion.

### THE JORDANIAN MILITARY

Because of Jordan's strategic importance in the turbulent Middle East, its military has always played a major role in society. With a total population of about 6 million, Jordan has 88,000 men in uniform. They are vital in a region that has been unstable for many years and could be called into action at any time. The king is the commander-in-chief of all the armed forces.

Jordanian Bedouin honor guards on the march. Jordan's military is small by the standards of its Middle East neighbors—in 2008 Jordan had about 88,000 soldiers on active duty, compared with 400,000 for Syria and 172,500 for Israel. However, the Jordanian Arab Army (originally called the Arab Legion) is considered among the best-trained forces in the region. Jordanian soldiers have participated in United Nations peacekeeping missions, such as those in Bosnia and Kosovo during the 1990s.

Military spending consumes approximately 25 percent of Jordan's national budget. Today, Saudi Arabia is the main supplier of funds for military equipment.

The Jordanian military has long been regarded as among the most competent in the Middle East. In the early years of the nation's existence as an independent state, the Jordanian military, called the Arab Legion, was considered the key supporter of the Hashemite monarchy. At first, the Arab Legion was made up of highly loyal Bedouins, whose salaries and equipment were paid for by Great Britain. Traditional martial attitudes among tribesmen and the opportunity for a secure career drew large numbers of the Bedouins into military service. Even today, most officers come from a Bedouin background.

Jordan requires a two-year military commitment from all men called to active duty. Students can defer active duty in order to continue their education, however.

Before the peace agreement of 1994, Jordan's post-1967 military strategy was based on the need to avoid facing Israel alone in a full-scale conflict. Jordan could not hope to prevail in such a war.

Reduced tensions with Israel have enabled military resources to be applied to the quest for domestic security. The militancy of the Islamic movement and the slow economic recovery in the 1990s after the Gulf War have made for unrest among certain elements of the Jordanian population.

Despite these issues, Jordan remains one of the most secure and stable countries in the region. It plays an important role not only in the Arab world, but in global politics as well.

# CHRONOLOGY

**8000 B.C.:** The Jordan River Valley is settled; evidence of first wheat cultivation in this area.

**4000 B.C.:** Ancient city of Jawa is established but eventually dies out, along with other urban cultures; nomads dominate the area.

**ca. 965 B.C.:** King David of the Hebrews expands his kingdom into the East Bank of the Jordan River, beginning 200 years of conflict between Hebrew armies and local tribal peoples.

**334 B.C.:** The Macedonian king Alexander the Great conquers the region.

**301 B.C.:** The Ptolemaic Empire, established in Egypt by one of Alexander's generals, takes control of the region and spreads classical Greek culture.

**ca. 200 B.C.:** The Nabatean kingdom, based in Petra, controls south Jordan region.

**ca. 100 B.C.:** The Roman Empire assumes control, annexing the kingdom of the Nabateans.

**ca. A.D. 50:** Christianity begins to spread throughout the region.

**395:** The Roman Empire splits into the Western Empire and the Eastern, or Byzantine, Empire, which is based in Constantinople; Byzantine Empire will control the Jordan region.

**ca. 570:** Muhammad, the Prophet of Islam, is born in Mecca.

**633:** Jordan region comes under the influence of Islamic armies moving northward from the Arabian Peninsula; ruling Islamic empires will include the Omayyads, Abbasids, Fatimids, and Seljuks.

**1099:** Armies of the First Crusade from Europe capture Jerusalem and establish a Christian kingdom that includes part of present-day Jordan.

**1187:** Saladin conquers Jerusalem and drives out the Crusaders; various Islamic empires based in Egypt will control this region.

**ca. 1550:** The Ottoman Empire takes over the region.

**ca. 1700:** Ottoman influence begins to decline as European powers grow stronger and begin to control the region's economy.

**1882:** Abdullah ibn Hussein, who will become the first king of Jordan, is born in Mecca.

**1914:** At the outbreak of World War I, Britain gives Arab nationalists vague promises for an Arab state in exchange for their support during the war.

# CHRONOLOGY

**1916:** The Arab Revolt against the Ottoman Empire begins.

**1918:** World War I ends; Ottomans have been defeated.

**1920:** The League of Nations conference in San Remo, Italy, establishes British mandate in Palestine and Iraq, and French mandate in Syria and Lebanon; Britain divides Palestine into Palestine and Transjordan.

**1921:** Britain gives Abdullah control of Transjordan.

**1928:** Anglo-Transjordan Agreement establishes basic constitution for Jordan, including a legislative council.

**1939:** World War II begins; Transjordan is an ally of Great Britain.

**1945:** The Arab League is founded, with Transjordan, Egypt, Syria, Lebanon, Saudi Arabia, Iraq, and Yemen as member states.

**1946:** Transjordan becomes the independent nation of Jordan and Abdullah is crowned king.

**1947:** The United Nations proposes a resolution for the establishment of separate Jewish and Arab states in Palestine; Jordan is the only Arab nation that votes in favor of this resolution.

**1948:** British forces pull out of Palestine; Jewish leaders declare the State of Israel; armies of the Arab League, including Jordan, attack the new nation but are ultimately defeated.

**1949:** Jordan signs truce with Israel; West Bank (including old city of Jerusalem) assigned as Palestinian territory, with Jordan exercising control.

**1950:** Jordan officially annexes West Bank.

**1951:** King Abdullah is assassinated by a Palestinian gunman enroute to a mosque in Jerusalem; his son, Talal, becomes king of Jordan.

**1952:** Talal abdicates his throne because he suffers from schizophrenia; Talal's son Hussein is named as regent.

**1953:** Hussein is crowned king of Jordan at age 18.

**1955:** Jordan joins the United Nations.

**1956:** King Hussein takes control of Jordan's armed forces, the Arab Legion, from the British.

**1964:** Palestine Liberation Organization (PLO) officially formed.

**1966:** King Hussein closes PLO offices in Amman.

**1967:** Israel defeats Arab countries, including Jordan, in the Six-Day War; Israel takes over West Bank.

**1968:** UN Resolution 242 is passed; resolution requires Israel to withdraw from occupied territories and Arabs to recognize State of Israel.

**1970:** A civil war between Jordanian armed forces and the PLO erupts in September; Jordanian forces win decisively, and the PLO eventually leaves Jordan.

**1974:** All Arab states except Jordan officially recognize the PLO as the legitimate representative of the Palestinian people.

**1978:** Egypt ratifies a peace treaty, called the Camp David Accords, with Israel; other Arab states, including Jordan, break off ties with Egypt.

**1984:** Jordan reestablishes diplomatic relations with Egypt.

**1987:** The *intifada*, or Palestinian uprising against Israel, begins in the West Bank.

**1988:** Jordan gives up its claim to the West Bank and supports the creation of a Palestinian state led by the PLO.

**1989:** Jordan holds legislative elections for the first time since the 1967 Six-Day War.

**1991:** Jordan remains neutral during the Gulf War, fought between a U.S.-led coalition and Iraq.

**1994:** Jordan and Israel sign a formal peace agreement.

**1999:** King Hussein dies of lymphatic cancer; his eldest son, Crown Prince Abdullah, becomes king of Jordan.

**2000:** Jordan joins the World Trade Organization.

**2002:** King Abdullah hosts an American delegation trying to work out a peace agreement between the PLO and Israel.

**2003:** Members of the Arab League meet in Bahrain.

**2005:** In March the ambassador to Israel returns after a four-year absence.

**2007:** The first elections are held since 1999. The main opposition party, the Islamic Action Front, withdraws and accuses the government of rigging the election.

**2008:** King Abdullah visits Iraq, becoming the first Arab leader to visit country after the U.S. invasion.

# GLOSSARY

**annexation**—the act of incorporating territory into a nation.

**Bedouin**—a member of an Arab tribe of the desert regions of North Africa or the Middle East who traditionally lived in tents and led a nomadic life following their herds.

**caliph**—a successor of Muhammad as religious and political leader of the Islamic empire.

**desalinization**—the process of removing salt from water so that it can be used for drinking or irrigation.

**East Bank**—the area of Jordan east of the Jordan River.

**emir**—a ruler, chief, or commander in an Islamic state.

**fedayeen**—Palestinian guerrilla fighters, especially those engaged in the struggle against Israel.

**gross domestic product (GDP)**—the total value of goods and services produced within a country in a one-year period.

**hajj**—the pilgrimage to Mecca, which every devout Muslim is supposed to try to make at least once in his or her lifetime.

**Hashemite**—a clan tracing its ancestry to Muhammad, whose members at one time had responsibility for the holy sites in Mecca and who founded the Hashemite dynasty in Jordan.

**Hejaz**—a region in the western part of modern-day Saudi Arabia that contains the Muslim holy cities of Medina and Mecca, and that was the original home of the Hashemite clan.

***intifada***—a violent Palestinian uprising against Israeli rule in the West Bank, beginning in late 1987; the Arabic word *intifada* may be translated as "shaking off."

**League of Nations**—an international organization established after World War I and designed to promote cooperation and peace among countries; it was the forerunner of the United Nations.

**mandate**—authorization to act that is given to a representative, specifically the authority given by the League of Nations to Great Britain and other European countries to establish governments in former colonies of Germany or other conquered areas after World War I.

***mukhtar***—the headman in an Arab village.

**nomadic**—having no permanent home but rather moving from place to place, often seasonally and within a defined territory.

**plateau**—an area of level land at a higher elevation than the surrounding land.

**remittances**—money earned by overseas workers that is sent back to support families in their home country.

***Sharia***—Islamic law.

**sheikh**—an Arab chief or tribal leader.

**sultan**—a king or sovereign of a Muslim state.

**Transjordan**—the region of Jordan east of the Jordan River, which was separated from Palestine under the British League of Nations mandate; the name Transjordan was originally given to the entire region of Jordan by the Ottoman Empire.

**Transjordanians**—residents of the area east of the Jordan River, or descended from those people.

**tributary**—a river or stream that flows into a larger river.

**wadi**—a canyon, valley, or streambed in a desert region that is usually dry but after a heavy rain will fill with water.

# FURTHER READING


Ashton, Nigel. *King Hussein of Jordan: A Political Life*. New Haven: Yale University Press, 2008.

Dallas, Roland. *King Hussein: A Life on the Edge*. New York: Fromm International Publishing, 1999.

*Hussein of Jordan, 1935–1999*. Amman, Jordan: King Hussein Foundation, 2000.

Lukacs, Yehuda. *Israel, Jordan, and the Peace Process*. Syracuse, N.Y.: Syracuse University Press, 1999.

Orbach, Benjamin. *Live From Jordan: Letters Home From My Journey Through the Middle East.* New York: AMACOM, 2007.

Paula, Christa. *Jordan: A Timeless Land.* London: I.B. Tauris, 2005.

Robins, Philip. *A History of Jordan.* London: Cambridge University Press, 2004.

Salibi, Kamil. *The Modern History of Jordan*. London: I. B. Taurus, 1998.

Shlaim, Avi. *Lion of Jordan: The Life of King Hussein in War and Peace*. New York: Knopf, 2008.

Surrat, Robin, ed. *The Middle East*, 9th ed. Washington, D.C.: Congressional Quarterly Press, 2000.

# INTERNET RESOURCES

**http://www.mideastinfo.com/jordan.htm**

Links to current news, a variety of Jordanian sites (government, education, business, media, and tourism), a country profile, and a map.

**http://www.jordanembassyus.org/**

Website of the Jordanian embassy in Washington, D.C., this site has extensive links to current news, as well as profiles of King Abdullah and Queen Rania, an archive of speeches and interviews with government leaders, and fact sheets on a wide range of information, including history, geography, culture, and politics.

**http://www.hejleh.com/countries/jordan.html**

This site offers a brief overview of Jordan's current political and economic situation and its history, as well as an extensive list of links to other sites.

**http://www.nic.gov.jo/**

Sponsored by the Jordanian National Information System, this site offers current statistical information gathered by Jordanian agencies.

**http://www.cia.gov/library/publications/the-world-factbook/geos/jo.html**

The CIA World Factbook's Jordan page provides up-to-date statistical information, divided into categories such as geography, people, economy, government, and communications.

**http://www.historycentral.com/nationbynation/Jordan/index.html**

Offers a brief overview as well as more detailed information on history, government, and human rights issues in Jordan.

**http://www.kinghussein.gov.jo**

A tribute site to King Hussein I of Jordan. Includes material on the country itself, including the people. population, and economy, as well as biographical material on Hussein.

# INDEX



Numbers in ***bold italic*** refer to captions.

# INDEX

# INDEX

# INDEX

# PICTURE CREDITS

2: © OTTN Publishing
3: Annie Griffiths Belt/Corbis
12: Richard T. Nowitz/Corbis
16: Jordanian Royal Palace via Getty Images
18: Nathan Benn/Corbis
20: Yann Arthus-Bertrand/Corbis
21: © OTTN Publishing
22: Dave G. Houser/Houserstock
26: Steve Kaufman/Corbis
27: Adam Woolfitt/Corbis
28: Dave G. Houser/Houserstock
31: Wolfgang Kaehler/Corbis
35: Ali Meyer/Corbis
36: Hulton/Archive/Getty Images
39: Bettmann/Corbis
42: Photo Disc
45: Hulton/Archive/Getty Images
46: Vittoriano Rastelli/Corbis
51: Scott Peterson/Liaison/Getty Images
52: Salah Malkawi/Newsmakers/Getty Images
56: National Press, Jordan
59: © OTTN Publishing
63: Francoise de Mulder/Corbis
64: Dave G. Houser/Houserstock
67: © OTTN Publishing
68: Richard T. Nowitz/Corbis
73: Lindsay Hebberd/Corbis
74: Salah Malkawi/Getty Images
75: Annie Griffiths Belt/Corbis
76: Reuters NewMedia Inc./Corbis
78: Charles & Josette Lenars/Corbis
81: Dave G. Houser/Houserstock
87: Owen Franken/Corbis
88: Peter Turnley/Corbis
91: Awad Awad/AFP/Getty Images
94: Eldad Rafaeli/Corbis
97: Alex Wong/Getty Images
98: Salah Malkawi/Getty Images

**Cover photos:** (both) PictureQuest

# CONTRIBUTORS

The **Foreign Policy Research Institute (FPRI)** served as editorial consultants for the Major Muslim Nations series. FPRI is one of the nation's oldest "think tanks." The Institute's Middle East Program focuses on Gulf security, monitors the Arab-Israeli peace process, and sponsors an annual conference for teachers on the Middle East, plus periodic briefings on key developments in the region.

Among the FPRI's trustees is a former Secretary of State and a former Secretary of the Navy (and among the FPRI's former trustees and interns, two current Undersecretaries of Defense), not to mention two university presidents emeritus, a foundation president, and several active or retired corporate CEOs.

The scholars of FPRI include a former aide to three U.S. Secretaries of State, a Pulitzer Prize–winning historian, a former president of Swarthmore College and a Bancroft Prize–winning historian, and two former staff members of the National Security Council. And the FPRI counts among its extended network of scholars—especially, its Inter-University Study Groups—representatives of diverse disciplines, including political science, history, economics, law, management, religion, sociology, and psychology.

**Dr. Harvey Sicherman** is president and director of the Foreign Policy Research Institute in Philadelphia, Pennsylvania. He has extensive experience in writing, research, and analysis of U.S. foreign and national security policy, both in government and out. He served as Special Assistant to Secretary of State Alexander M. Haig Jr. and as a member of the Policy Planning Staff of Secretary of State James A. Baker III. Dr. Sicherman was also a consultant to Secretary of the Navy John F. Lehman Jr. (1982–1987) and Secretary of State George Shultz (1988).

A graduate of the University of Scranton (B.S., History, 1966), Dr. Sicherman earned his Ph.D. at the University of Pennsylvania (Political Science, 1971), where he received a Salvatori Fellowship. He is author or editor of numerous books and articles, including *America the Vulnerable: Our Military Problems and How to Fix Them* (FPRI, 2002) and *Palestinian Autonomy, Self-Government and Peace* (Westview Press, 1993). He edits *Peacefacts*, an FPRI bulletin that monitors the Arab-Israeli peace process.

**Anna Carew-Miller**, a freelance writer and former teacher, lives in northwestern Connecticut with her husband and daughter. Although she has a Ph.D. in American Literature and has done extensive research and writing on literary topics, more recently Anna has written books for younger readers, including reference books and middle-reader mysteries.